THE BURNS QUOTATION BOOK

By the same editors

The Scottish Quotation Book
The Music Quotation Book
The Theatre & Opera-lover's Quotation Book

The
Burns Quotation
Book

Edited by
JOYCE AND MAURICE LINDSAY

ROBERT HALE · LONDON

Preface and selection © Joyce and Maurice Lindsay 1994
First published in Great Britain 1994

ISBN 0 7090 5287 1

Robert Hale Limited
Clerkenwell House
Clerkenwell Green
London EC1R 0HT

The right of Joyce and Maurice Lindsay to be identified as
authors of this work has been asserted by them
in accordance with the Copyright, Designs and
Patents Act 1988.

2   4   6   8   10   9   7   5   3   1

Photoset in Garamond by
Derek Doyle & Associates, Mold, Clwyd.
Printed and bound in Great Britain by
WBC Ltd, Bridgend, Mid-Glamorgan.

Preface

This book has several possible uses. Firstly, it may induce some readers unfamiliar with Burns's poetry, or, more particularly, with his letters, to seek out the originals for further reading. The ur-texts *are* The Poems and Songs of Robert Burns, *edited by James Kinsley (1968) and* The Letters of Robert Burns, *edited by G. Ross Roy (1985). Biographies of the characters in the Burns story are to be found in* The Burns Encyclopaedia.

Secondly, this book is, inevitably, to some extent autobiographical; indeed, might well have been subtitled Burns by Himself.

Thirdly, and what will probably be its most frequent use, it is a kind of vade-mecum *for all those who, at least once in their lives, find themselves called upon to speak at a Burns supper.*

Fourthly, so pointed is Burns's wisdom on many aspects of life, that, like most anthologies, it can do duty as a rewarding dip-into book by the bedside. All those who knew Burns testified to his keen intelligence. He is never less than interesting, often much more.

He was not, of course, the unlettered heaven-taught ploughman that some of the Edinburgh literati liked to think him, notably Henry Mackenzie, though Burns sometimes assumed that mantle in his periodic role-playing (the rural rustic for the aristocracy, the military aspirant or the devout religionist for Mrs Dunlop). The evidence of his reading shows him to have been well read, if not systematically so. In religion he was a reluctant Deist, observing, 'I hate a man that wishes to be a Deist, but I fear, every fair, un-prejudiced enquirer must in some degree be a Sceptic.' Dogmas he despised, but he would dearly have liked to believe in the likelihood of an afterlife, though he could not for long silence his doubts. In philosophy he was much influenced by the empiricism of Locke's An Essay Concerning Human Understanding *(1689) and by the 'Common Sense' philosophy expressed in Thomas Reid's unconvincing attempt to refute Hume,* An Inquiry Into The Human Mind *(1764). There is no evidence that Burns actually read Hume's* A Treatise of Human Nature *(1739–40), though plenty to suggest that he was not untouched by the philosopher's antipathy to dogma, his scepticism and systematic empiricism. In politics, Burns was a sentimental Jacobite, affected by a romantic nostalgia that hung about the poetic air into the early nineteenth-century years of James Hogg and Lady Nairne. He deeply regretted the loss of Scottish independence, brought about by the Act of Union of 1707 and the attempt of some of his contemporaries to de-Scotticize the Scottish tongue and turn the country into North Britain.*

On the wider political front, his hatred of empty rank and meritless privilege undoubtedly echoed the principles set out in Thomas Paine's The Rights of Man *(1791 & 2). Like the young Wordsworth, Burns saw fresh hope for humanity in the early manifestation of the French Revolution; but Jacobinism soon frightened those in British authority. Burns was the eighteenth-century equivalent of a civil servant, and therefore, as is still the case today, muzzled. Some of the growls that* nevertheless escaped the muzzle got him into official trouble, forcing him to write crawling letters to protect his family's daily bread-and-butter.

As a poet, he was a consummate craftsman who thought deeply about his art. Like many great artists he was not primarily an innovator, preferring to take up existing forms and fashion them to more telling effect than any of his predecessors had done. As a song-writer, and song-refurbisher, he was probably helped by having some elementary skill on the violin, which he possibly played 'by ear'. There is some slight evidence in one of his letters to James Johnson, however, suggesting that he may have been familiar with the rudiments of musical notation. His musical taste and sureness of judgement were confined to folk airs, in which his sense of matching fitness was unerring. His folk-song work for Johnson and, later for George Thomson, gave him great satisfaction and occupied him increasingly in his final years, when his output of occasional social verses also increased. After Tam O'Shanter, indeed, nearly all that was great came from him in song form.

The exhausting business of riding some two hundred miles a week on his excise affairs and, after he had moved to a Dumfries foot-walk division, his increasing drinking, took their toll on his health and creativity. It might be thought, as I once supposed, that a man in the 1790s on a salary of £70 a year, later reduced by at least £20 because of the conditions created by the war with France, would not have been able to afford to drink heavily; but it was a hard-drinking age, and Burns himself observed, latterly his drinking did not so much take place in taverns as in the houses of the gentry, where he was a frequent guest. His sober-minded brother, Gilbert, denied that he drank too much; but his great friend Maria Riddell, though the authoress of a prompt and generous *posthumous memoir of her poet friend, refused, however, to be an apologist for 'the irregularities even of a man of genius'.*

His attitude to women was ambiguous. With his 'mother-confessor' Mrs Dunlop; with Mrs Maria Riddell and, to some extent, with Margaret Chalmers, what he enjoyed was primarily intellectual friendship, no doubt spiced, so far as the two younger women were concerned, with a certain latent sexual frisson. *Yet there is plenty of evidence to suggest that on a lower social level, he regarded women primarily as, in our late twentieth-century phrase, 'sex objects'.*

Burns caught the traditional independent ethos of the old agrarian Scotland just as the distance-delayed effects of the Union of 1707 and the onslaught of the Industrial Revolution were about to change things for ever. To Scots he expresses what they see as fundamental 'national values' gone beyond recall, often with a kind of compressed proverbial wisdom that makes them easily memorable. His understanding of human nature, particularly of the relationship between men and women from virginal girlhood to long-married old age, has helped to give him the status of a world poet, translated into countless languages. After Dante, Shakespeare and Goethe, he may well rank fourth in the pantheon of the world's literary 'greats'.

In The Burns Quotation Book, *entries are arranged alphabetically by subject matter. That Burns himself approved of quotations is evidenced by his views on them, found under the letter Q. Obviously, not everything quotable which Burns wrote or said could be included, but we have tried to range widely over the subjects that engaged his perceptive attention.*

We have quoted from the poems and songs found in the Kinsley edition. This includes some older songs which

Burns simply altered and improved; those numbers of The Merry Muses *(not so titled by Burns) regarded as his work and such fairly convincing attributions in style, content and tone as* The Tree of Liberty. *We have, however, used modern spelling (i.e. 'favour' instead of Burns's pre-Shavian 'favor') and corrected such obvious errors as Johnson for Jonson.*

JOYCE AND MAURICE LINDSAY

Aim

The great misfortune of my life was, never to have An Aim.

to Dr John Moore, 30 June 1787

America

I dare say, the American Congress, in 1766, will be allowed to have been as able and as enlightened, and, a whole empire will say, as honest, as the English Convention in 1688; and that the fourth of July will be as sacred to their posterity as the fifth of November is to us.

to the Editor of the *Edinburgh Evening Courant*, 8 November 1788

Is it not remarkable, odiously remarkable, that tho' manners are more civilized, and the rights of mankind better understood, by an Augustan Century's improvement, yet in this very reign of heavenly Hanoverianism … an empire beyond the Atlantic has had its Revolution too, and for the very same maladministration and legislative misdemeanours in the illustrious and sapienipotent Family of Hanover as was complained of in the 'tyrannical and bloody house of Stuart'.

to Mrs Dunlop, 13 November 1788

Animals

Ca' the yowes to the knowes,
    Ca' them whare the heather grows,

11

Ca' them whare the burnie rowes,
    My bonie Dearie.
  'Ca' the Yowes to the Knowes'

Wee, sleeket, cowran' tim'rous beastie,
O, what a panic's in thy breastie!
Thou needna start awa sae hasty,
    Wi' bickering brattle!
I wad be laith to rin an' chase thee,
    Wi' murd'ring pattle!

I'm truly sorry Man's dominion
Has broken Nature's social union,
An' justifies that ill opinion,
    Which makes thee startle
At me, thy poor, earth-born companion,
    An' fellow mortal! …

But Mousie, thou art no thy lane,
In proving *foresight* may be vain;
The best laid schemes o' Mice an' Men,
    Gang aft agley,
An' lea'e us nought but grief an' pain,
    For promis'd joy!
  'To a Mouse, on turning her up in her Nest, with the
        Plough', November 1785

He was a gash an' faithfu' tyke,
As ever lap a sheugh, or dyke,
His honest, sonsie, baws'nt face,
Ay gat him friends in ilka place;
His breast was white, his towzie back
Weel clad wi' coat o' glossy black;
His gawsie tail, wi' upward curl,
Hung owre his hurdies wi' a swirl.
  'The Twa Dogs'

That damned mare of yours is dead. I would freely have
given her price to have saved her ... I took every care of
her in my power. She was never crossed for riding above
half a score of times by me or in my keeping. I drew her
in the plough, one of three, for one poor week. I
refused fifty-five shillings for her, which was the highest
bode I could squeeze for her. I fed her up and had her in
fine order for Dumfries fair; when four or five days
before the fair, she was seized with an unaccountable
disorder in her sinews, or somewhere in the bones of her
neck; with a weakness of total want of power in her
fillets; and, in short, the vertebrae of her spine seemed to
be diseased and unhinged; and in eight and forty hours,
in spite of the two best farriers in the country, she died
and be damned to her! The farriers said she had been
quite strained in the fillets beyond cure before you had
bought her ... While she was with me ... I assure you,
my much valued friend, everything was done for her that
could be done; and the accident has vexed me to the
heart.

to William Nicol, 9 February 1790

Peg Nicholson was a good bay mare,
    As ever trod on airn;
But now she's floating down the Nith
    And past the Mouth o' Cairn ...

Peg Nicholson was a good bay mare,
    And aince she bore a priest;
But now she's floating down the Nith,
    For Solway fish a feast.

Peg Nicholson was a good bay mare,
    And the priest he rode her sair;

And much oppressed and bruised she was –
  As priest-rid cattle are.
'Elegy on Peg Nicholson'

We proceeded to spend the day on Loch Lomond, and reached Dumbarton in the evening. We dined at another fellow's house, and consequently, pushed the bottle; when we went out to mount our horses, we found ourselves 'No vera fou but gaylie, yet'. My two friends and I rode soberly down the Loch side, till by came a Highlandman at a gallop, on a tolerably good horse, but which had never known the ornaments of iron or leather. We scorned to be out-galloped by a Highlandman, so off we started, whip and spur. My companions, though seemingly gaily mounted, fell sadly astern; but my old mare, Jenny Geddes, one of the Rosinante family, strained past the Highlandman in spite of all his efforts with the hair halter; just as I was passing him, Donald wheeled his horse, as if to cross before me to mar my progress, when down came his horse, and threw his rider's breekless a-e in a clipt hedge; and down came Jenny Geddes over all, and my Bardship between her and the Highlandman's horse. Jenny Geddes trode over me with such cautious reverence, that matters were not so bad as might well have been expected; so I came off with a few cuts and bruises, and a thorough resolution to be a pattern of sobriety for the future.
  to James Smith, 30 June 1787

Two mornings ago as I was, at a very early hour, sowing the fields, I heard a shot, and presently a poor little hare limped by me, apparently very much hurt. You will easily guess, this set my humanity in tears, and my indignation in arms. The following was the result:

Inhuman Man! curse on thy barb'rous art,
    And blasted be thy murder-aiming eye;
    May never pity soothe thee with a sigh,
Nor ever pleasure glad thy cruel heart!

Go live, poor wanderer of the wood and field,
    The bitter little that of life remains:
    No more the thickening brakes and verdant
        plains
To thee shall home, or food, or pastime yield.

Seek, mangled wretch, some place of wonted rest,
    No more of rest, but now thy dying bed!
    The sheltering rushes whistling o'er thy head,
The cold earth with thy bloody bosom prest ...
  'On Seeing a Wounded Hare Limp by Me'
  to Mrs Dunlop, 21 April 1789

I have always had an abhorrence at this way of assassinating God's creatures without first allowing them those means of defence with which he has variously endowed them; but at this season when the object of our treacherous murder is most probably a Parent, perhaps the mother, and of consequence to leave two little hapless nurslings to perish with hunger amidst the pitiless wilds, such an action is not only a sin against the letter of the law, but likewise a deep crime against the *morality of the heart*.
  to Patrick Miller, 21 June 1789

Authors
The first books I met with in my early years ... were the lives of Hannibal and Sir William Wallace. For several of my earlier years I had few other Authors; and many a solitary hour have I stole out, after the laborious

vocations of the day, to shed a tear over their glorious but unfortunate Story.

to Mrs Dunlop, 15 November 1786

Two stray volumes of Pamela, and one of Ferdinand, Count Fathom ... gave me some idea of novels. Rhyme, except some religious pieces which are in print, I had given up; but meeting with Fergusson's Scotch Poems, I strung anew my wildly-sounding, rustic lyre with emulating vigour.

to Dr John Moore, August 1787

I want a Shakespeare ... I likewise want an English dictionary; Johnson's I suppose is best.

to Peter Hill, 2 April 1789

I want only, Books; the cheapest way, the best ... I want Smollett's works, for the sake of his incomparable humour. I have already Roderick Random and Humphry Clinker. Peregrine Pickle, Launcelot Greaves and Ferdinand Count Fathom, I still want; but ... the veriest ordinary copies will serve me. I am nice only in the appearance of my Poets. I forget the price of Cowper's Poems, but I believe I must have them!

to Peter Hill, 18 July 1788

I want ... for myself, as you pick them up second-handed or any way cheap copies of Otway's dramatic works, Ben Jonson's, Dryden's, Congreve's, Wycherly's, Vanbrugh's, Cibber's, or any dramatic works of the more Moderns, Macklin, Garrick, Foote, Colman or Sheridan's. A good copy too of Molière in French I much want; Corneille, and Voltaire too. I am in no hurry for all or any of these, but if you accidentally meet with them very cheap, get them for me.

to Peter Hill, 2 March 1790

Your books have delighted me; Virgil, Dryden, and Tasso, were all equally strangers to me!

to Mrs Dunlop, 28 April 1788

Dryden's Virgil has delighted me. I do not know whether the critics will agree, but the Georgics are to me by far the best of Virgil. It is indeed a species of writing entirely new to me, and has filled my head with a thousand fancies of emulation ... I am disappointed in the Aeneid ... I think Virgil, in many instances, a servile copier of Homer. If I had the Odyssey by me, I could parallel many passages where Virgil has evidently copied, but by no means improved, Homer. Nor can I think there is anything of this owing to the translators; for, from everything I have seen of Dryden, I think him, in genius and fluency of language, Pope's master.

to Mrs Dunlop, 4 May 1788

Cowper's poems, the best poet out of sight since Thomson.

to William Dunbar, 25 September 1788

How do you like Cowper? Is not The Task a glorious Poem? The Religion of The Task, bating a few scraps of Calvinistic Divinity, is the religion of God and Nature; the Religion that exalts, that ennobles Man.

to Mrs Dunlop, 15 December 1793

My favourite authors are of the sentimental kind, such as Shenstone, particularly his Elegies, Thomson, Man of Feeling, a book I prize next to the Bible, Man of the World, Sterne, especially his Sentimental Journey, Macpherson's Ossian and etc. These are the glorious models after which I endeavour to form my conduct.

to John Murdoch, 15 January 1783

The periods of Johnson and the pauses of Sterne may hide a selfish heart.

> to Mrs Dunlop, 15 April 1787

In justice to Spenser I must acknowledge that there is scarcely a poet in the language could have been a more agreeable present to me.

> to William Dunbar, 30 April 1787

O Pope, had I thy satire's darts
to gie the rascals their deserts,
I'd rip their rotten, hollow hearts
    And tell aloud
Their jugglin' hocus-pocus arts
     To cheat the crowd.

> 'To the Reverend John M'Math'

Thou canst not learn, nor can I show,
To paint with Thomson's landscape glow;
Or wake the bosom-melting throe,
    With Shenstone's art;
Or pour, with Gray, the moving flow
     Warm on the heart.

> (Coila, Burns's Muse, addresses the Poet)
> 'The Vision'

My senses wad be in a creel,
Should I but dare a hope to speel,
Wi' Allan, or wi' Gilbertfield,
    The braes o' fame;
Or Fergusson, the writer-chiel,
    A deathless name.

(O Fergusson! thy glorious parts,
Ill-suited law's dry, musty arts!

My curse upon your whunstane hearts,
    Ye E'nbrugh gentry.
The tythe o' what ye waste at cartes
    Wad stow'd his pantry).
   'To William Simson'

Ramsay, as every other Poet, has not always been equally happy in his pieces; still, I cannot approve of taking such liberties with an Author as Mr Walker proposes doing with 'The last time I came o'er the moor'. Let a Poet, if he chooses, take up the idea of another, and work it into a piece of his own; but to mangle the works of the poor Bard whose tuneful tongue is now mute for ever in the dark and narrow house, by Heaven 'twould be sacrilege!
    to George Thomson, April 1793

Poor Fergusson! If there be a life beyond the grave, which I trust there is; and if there be a good God presiding over all nature, which I am sure there is; thou art now enjoying existence in a glorious world where worth of the heart alone is distinction in the man; where riches deprived of all their pleasure-purchasing powers, return to their native sordid matter; where titles and honours are the disregarded reveries of an idle dream; and where that heavy virtue, which is the negative consequence of steady dulness, and whose thoughtless though often destructive follies, which are the unavoidable aberrations of frail human nature, will be thrown into equal oblivion, as if they had never been!
    to Peter Stuart, August 1789

I send you by the bearer, Mr Clarke, a particular friend of mine, six pounds and a shilling, which you will dispose of as follows: £5–10, per account I owe Mr

Robert Burn, Architect, for erecting the stone over poor Fergusson. He was two years in erecting it, after I commissioned him for it; and I have been two years paying him, after he sent me his account; so he and I are quits. He had the hardiesse to ask me interest on the sum; but considering that the money was due by one Poet, for putting a tomb-stone over another, he may, with grateful surprise, thank Heaven that he ever saw a farthing of it.

> to Peter Hill, 5 February 1792

No sculptured marble here, nor pompous lay,
    'No storied urn nor animated bust';
This simple stone directs pale Scotia's way,
    To pour her sorrows o'er the Poet's dust.

> Inscription for the Headstone of Fergusson the Poet

Give me a spirit like my favourite hero, Milton's Satan.

> to James Smith, 11 June 1787

My favourite feature in Milton's Satan is, his manly fortitude in supporting what cannot be remedied – in short, the wild broken fragments of a noble, exalted mind in ruins.

> to Mrs Agnes M'Lehose, 5 January 1788

Whatever Milton had, I have no idea of a Cherub six feet high.

> to William Dunbar, 25 September 1788

Solomon's knowledge of the world is very great. He may be looked on as the 'Spectator' or 'Adventurer' of his day; and it is, indeed, surprising what a sameness has ever been in human nature.

> to Mrs M'Lehose, 1 February 1788

Mackenzie has been called the Addison of the Scots, and in my opinion, Addison would not be hurt by the comparison.

to Mrs Dunlop, 10 April 1790

I inclose you, for Mr Boswell, the Ballad you mentioned; and as I hate sending waste paper or mutilating a sheet, I have filled it up with one or two of my fugitive Pieces ... Should they procure me the honour of being introduced to Mr Boswell, I shall think they have great merit. There are few pleasures my late will-o'-the-wisp character has given me equal to that of having seen many of the extraordinary men, the Heroes of Wit and Literature in my Country; and as I had the honour of drawing first breath almost in the same Parish with Mr Boswell, my Pride plumes itself on the connection ... to have been acquainted with such a man as Mr Boswell, I would hand down to my Posterity as one of the honours of their ancestor.

to Bruce Campbell, 13 November 1788

Falconer, the poor unfortunate Author of the Shipwreck, that glorious Poem which you so much admire, is no more. After weathering that dreadful catastrophe he so feelingly describes in his Poem, and after weathering many hard gales of Fortune, he went to the bottom with the Aurora frigate! I forget what part of Scotland had the honour of giving him birth, but he was the son of obscurity and misfortune. He was one of these daring adventurous spirits which old Caledonia beyond any other nation is remarkable for producing.

to Mrs Dunlop, 25 January 1790

You are right, Madam, in your idea of poor Mylne's poem, which he has addressed to me. The piece has a good deal of merit, but it has one damning fault – it is by

far too long. Besides, my success has encouraged such a shoal of ill-spawned monsters to crawl into public notice, under the title of Scots Poets, that the very term, Scots Poetry, borders on the burlesque.
> to Mrs Dunlop, 4 March 1789

It is not easy forming an exact judgement on anyone, but in my opinion Dr Blair is merely an astonishing proof of what industry and application can do.
> *Second Commonplace Book*

Light be the turf on the breast of the heaven-inspired Poet who composed this glorious Fragment! ['Auld Lang Syne']. There is more of the fire of native genius in it, than in half a dozen of modern English Bacchanalians.
> to Mrs Dunlop, 7 December 1788

Birds

The Robin cam to the wren's nest
    And keekit in, and keekit in,
O weel's me on your auld pow,
    Wad ye be in, wad ye be in.
Ye'se ne'er get leave to lie without,
    And I within, and I within,
As lang's I hae an auld clout,
    To row you in, to row you in.
> 'The Wren's Nest'

Rejoice, ye birring pairtricks a';
Ye cootie muircocks, crously craw;
Ye maukins, cock your fud fu' braw
    Withouten dreid;
Your mortal fae is now awa' –
    Tam Samson's deid.
> 'Tam Samson's Elegy'

Now westlin winds and slaught'ring guns
 Bring Autumn's pleasant weather;
The moorcock springs on whirring wings
 Amang the blooming heather …

The pairtrick loves the fruitfu' fells,
 The plover lo'es the mountains;
The woodcock haunts the lanely dells,
 The soaring hern the fountains;
Thro' lofty groves the cushat roves,
 The path of men to shun it;
The hazel bush o'erhangs the thrush
 The spreading thorn the linnet.
 'Now Westlin Winds'

'Twas when the stacks got on their winter-hap,
And thack and rape secure the toil-won crap;
Potato-bings are sugged up frae skaith
Of coming Winter's biting, frosty breath;
The bees, rejoicing o'er their summer toils,
Unnumber'd buds an' flow'rs delicious spoils,
Seal'd up with frugal care in massive waxen piles,
Are doom'd by Man, that tyrant o'er the weak,
The death o' devils, smoor'd wi' brimstane reek;
The thund'ring guns are heard on ev'ry side,
The wounded coveys reeling, scatter wide;
The feather'd field-mates, bound by Nature's tie,
Sires, mothers, children, in one carnage lie:
(What warm, poetic heart but inly bleeds,
And execrates man's savage, ruthless deeds!)
Nae mair the flow'r in field or meadow springs,
Nae mair the grove with airy concert rings,
Except, perhaps, the Robin's whistling glee,
Proud o' the height o' some bit half-lang tree …
 'The Brigs of Ayr'

The sober laverock, warbling wild,
    Shall to the skies aspire;
The gowdspink, Music's gayest child,
    Shall sweetly join the choir;
The blackbird strong, the lintwhite clear,
    The mavis mild and mellow;
The robin pensive Autumn cheer,
    In all her locks of yellow.
  'The Humble Petition of Bruar Water'

The eagle, from the cliffy brow,
Marking you his prey below,
In his breast no pity dwells,
Strong Necessity compels;
But Man, to whom alone is giv'n
A ray direct from pitying Heaven,
Glories in his heart humane –
And creatures for his pleasures slain.
  'On Scaring some Water-fowl by Loch Turit'

The simple bard, rough at the rustic plough,
Learning his tuneful trade from ev'ry bough;
The chanting linnet, or the mellow thrush,
Hailing the setting sun, sweet, in the green thorn
      bush,
The soaring lark, the perching red-breast shrill,
Or deep-ton'd plovers, grey, wild-whistling o'er the
      hill …
  'The Brigs of Ayr'

Books

Through and through the inspired leaves,
    Ye maggots, make your windings;
But, oh, respect his lordship's taste,
    And spare his golden bindings.
  'The Book Worms'

Booksellers

I believe Booksellers take no less than the unconscionable, Jewish tax of 25 prcent. by way of agency.

to John Ballantine, 18 April 1787

Character

Have you ever met a perfect character? Do we not sometimes rather exchange faults than get rid of them?

to Mrs M'Lehose, 4 January 1788

Strange! how apt we are to indulge prejudices in our judgement of one another! Even I, who pique myself on my skill in marking characters; because I am too proud of my character as a man, to be dazzled in my judgement *for* glaring wealth; and too proud of my situation as a poor man to be biassed *against* squalid poverty.

to Margaret Chalmers, 7 April 1788

A flatterer ... next to a backbiter is the most detestable character under the sun.

to William Niven, 29 July 1780

Clothes

The mother wi' her needle an' her shears,
Gars auld claes look amaist as weel's the new.

'The Cottar's Saturday Night'

... send me by the bearer, John Ronald, carrier between Glasgow and Mauchline, fifteen yards of black silk, the same kind as that of which I bought a gown and petticoat from you formerly – Lutestring, I think is its name – I shall send you the money and a more coherent letter, when he goes again to your good town.

to Robert M'Indoe, 5 August 1788

In order that you may have the higher idea of my merits in this momentous affair, I must tell you that all the haberdashers here are on the alarm as to the necessary article of French gloves. You must know that French gloves are contraband goods, and expressly forbidden by the laws of this wisely-governed realm of ours. A satirist would say that this is the reason why the ladies are so fond of them; but I, who have not one grain of *Gall* in my composition, shall allege that it is the patriotism of the dear goddess of man's idolatry that makes them so fond of dress from the land of Liberty and Equality.... I have discovered one haberdasher who, at my particular request, will clothe your fair hands as they ought to be, to keep them from being profaned by the rude gaze of the gloating eye, or – horrid! – from perhaps a [kiss] by the unhallowed lips of the satyr Man.

to Mrs Maria Riddell, April 1793

Conscience

There is nothing in the whole frame of man, which seems to me so unaccountable as that thing called conscience. Had the troublesome yelping cur powers efficient to prevent a mischief, he might be of use; but at the beginning of the business, his feeble efforts are to the workings of passion as the infant frosts of an autumnal morning to the unclouded fervour of the rising sun; and no sooner are the tumultuous doings of the wicked deed over, than, amidst the bitter native consequences of folly, in the very vortex of our horrors, up starts conscience and harrows us with the feelings of the damned.

to Peter Stuart, February, 1787

Conversation

I don't know how it is with the world in general, but with me, making remarks is by no means a solitary pleasure. I want someone to laugh with me, someone to be grave with me; someone to please me and help my discrimination with his or her own remark, and at times, no doubt, to admire my acuteness and penetration.

Second Commonplace Book

Correspondence

Answer a letter? I never could answer a letter in my life! I have witten many a letter in return for letters I have received; but then – they were original matter – spurt – away! zig, here; zag there ...

to Robert Ainslie, 26 April 1793

Though I never sit down to *answer* a letter, as our Pastoral Bards make their contending Swains answer one another, or as a be-periwigged Edinburgh Advocate answers his begowned brother, yet I cannot help thanking you particularly for the poetic compliment in your epistle the last I received but one.

to Mrs Dunlop, 23 October 1788

I have long since given up that kind of formal correspondence, where one sits down irksomely to write a letter, because we think we are in duty bound to do so.

to William Dunbar, 7 April 1788

The hurry of a farmer in this particular season and the indolence of a poet at all times and seasons will, I hope, plead my excuse for neglecting so long to answer your obliging letter ...

to Peter Stuart, August 1789

How can you expect a Correspondent should write you when you declare that you mean to preserve his letters with a view, sooner or later, to expose them on the pillory of derision and the rack of criticism?

to Mrs Agnes M'Lehose, July 1791

Old as I am in acquaintance, and growing grey in connection, with Slips, Frips, Failings, Frailties, Back-slidings in the paths of grace, and Forward fa's upon a naked wame, and all the other lighthorse militia of iniquity, never did my poor back suffer such sacrification from the scourge of conscience, as during these three weeks that your kind epistle has lain by me unanswered.

to William Corbet, September 1792

I am two kind letters in your debt, but I have been from home, and horribly busy buying and preparing for that farming business; over and above the plague of my Excise Instructions which this week will finish.

to Robert Ainslie, 26 May 1788

I admire the close of a letter Lord Bolinbroke wrote to Dean Swift: 'Adieu, dear Swift! With all thy faults well I love thee; make an effort and love me with all mine.' Humble servant, etc., all that trumpery, is now such a perversion, such a Sodomy of Language, that Honest Friendship, in her sincere way, must have recourse to simple, Farewell!

to Robert Ainslie, 30 June 1788

When I write you, Madam, I do not sit down to answer every paragraph of yours, by echoing every sentiment – like, the faithful Commons of Great Britain, in parliament assembled, answering a speech from the best of Kings! I just write in the fulness of my heart, and may perhaps be guilty of neglecting some of your kind inquiries – but not from your very odd reason that I do not read your letters.

to Mrs Dunlop, 10 August 1788

I am no dab at fine-drawn letter-writing; and, except when prompted by friendship or gratitude, or, which happens extremely rarely, inspired by the Muse (I know not her name) that presides over epistolary writing, I sit down, when necessitated to write, as I would sit down to beat hemp.

to Mrs Dunlop, 6 September 1789

Now that my first sentence is concluded, I have nothing to do but to pray Heaven to help me to another. Shall I write you on Politics, or Religion, two master-subjects for your Sayers of nothing?

to Provost Robert Maxwell, 20 December 1789

Since we are creatures of a day, since a 'few summer days, and a few winter nights, and the life of man is at an end', why, dear much-esteemed Sir, should you and I let negligent indolence, for I know it is nothing worse, step in between us, and bar the enjoyment of a mutual correspondence? We are not shapen out of the common, heavy, methodical Clod, the elemental Stuff of the plodding, selfish Race, the sons of Arithmetic and Prudence; our feelings and hearts are not benumbed and poisoned by the cursed influence of riches, which, whatever blessing they may be in other respects, are no friends to the nobler qualities of the heart; in the name of random Sensibility, then, let never the moon change on our silence anymore.

to William Dunbar, 14 January 1790

No! I will not say one word about apologies or excuses for not writing you. I am a poor, damn'd rascally Gager, condemned to gallop at least 200 miles every week to inspect dirty ponds and yeasty barrels, and where can I find time, or importance to interest, anybody?

to Peter Hill, 2 February 1790

I can *antithesize* Sentiment and *circumvolute* Periods, as well as any Coiner of phrase in the regions of Philology.
to Alexander Cunningham, 13 February 1790

Were it not for our gracious monarch's cursed tax of postage, I had sent you one or two Pieces of some length that I have lately done.
to Robert Cleghorn, 23 January 1789

Criticism and Critics

You are right in your guesses that I am not very amenable to counsel. Poets, much my superiors, have so flattered those who possessed the adventitious qualities of wealth and power that I am determined to flatter no created being in prose or verse, so help me God ... I set as little by kings, lords, clergy, critics ... as all these respectable Gentry do by my Bardship.
to Mrs Dunlop, 30 April 1787

Your Criticisms, my honoured Benefactress, are truly the work of a Friend. They are not the blasting depredations of a canker-toothed, caterpillar-Critic; nor are they the fair statement of cold Impartiality, balancing with unfeeling exactitude the pro and con of an Author's merits; they are the judicious observations of animated Friendship, selecting the beauties of the Piece.
to Mrs Dunlop, 27 September 1788

Faultless correctness may please, and does highly please, the lettered critic; but to that awful character I have not the most distant pretensions.
to Mrs Dunlop, 4 May 1788

Your critic – folk may cock their nose,
An' say, 'How can you e'er propose,
You wha ken hardly verse frae prose,
    To mak a sang?'
But, by your leave, my learned foes,
    Ye're maybe wrang.
    'Epistle to John Lapraik'

Critics – appalled, I venture on the name,
Those cut-throat bandits in the paths of fame;
Bloody dissectors, worse than ten Monroes;
He hacks to teach, they mangle to expose.
    'The Poet's Progress'

Damn the pedant, frigid soul of Criticism for ever and ever!

    to Gavin Hamilton, Edinburgh, 8 March 1787

... if these mortals, the Critics, should bustle,
I care not, not I, let the Critics go whistle!
    'Sketch'
    (Inscribed to the Rt. Hon. Charles J. Fox Esq)

The worst of it is, by the time one has finished a piece, it has been so often viewed and reviewed before the mental eye, that one loses in a good measure the powers of critical discrimination. Here the best criterion I know is a friend, not only of abilities to judge, but with good-nature enough, like a prudent teacher with a young learner, to praise perhaps a little more than is exactly just, lest the thin-skinned animal fall into that most deplorable of all poetic diseases – heart-breaking despondency of himself.

    to Dr John Moore, 4 January 1789

I would not give a farthing for a book, unless I were at liberty to blot it with my criticism.

    to Mrs Dunlop, 15 December 1793

Dancing

In my seventeenth year, to give my manners a brush, I
went to a country dancing school. My father had an
unaccountable antipathy against these meetings; and my
going was, what to this hour I repent, in absolute
defiance of his commands.

> to Dr John Moore, Mauchline, 2 August 1787

There's threesome reels, there's foursome reels,
    There's hornpipes and strathspeys, man,
But the ae best dance e'er cam to the land,
    Was the deil's awa wi' the Exciseman.
'The Deil's Awa wi' the Exciseman'

At a Highland gentleman's hospitable mansion, we fell
in with a merry party, and danced till the ladies left us, at
three in the morning. Our dancing was none of the
French or English insipid formal movements ... we flew
at Bab at the Bowster, Tullochgorum, Loch Erroch Side,
etc., like midges sporting in the mottie sun, or craws
prognosticating a storm in a hairst day.

> to James Smith, 30 June 1787

Death

Poets have in this the same advantage as Roman
Catholics; they can be of service to their friends after
they have passed that bourne where all other kindness
ceases to be of any avail. Whether after all, either the one
or the other be of any real service to the Dead is, I fear,
very problematical...

> to Dr John Moore, 28 February 1791

O what is death but parting breath?
    On many a bloody plain
I've dared his face, and in this place
    I scorn him yet again.
'M'Pherson's Farewell'

Is it departing pangs my soul alarms?
    Or death's unlovely, dreary, dark abode?
For guilt, for guilt, my terrors are in arms:
    I tremble to approach an angry God,
And justly smart beneath his sin-avenging rod.
    'Stanzas in the Prospect of Death'

O Death! the poor man's dearest friend,
    The kindest and the best!
Welcome the hour my aged limbs
    Are laid with thee to rest!
The great, the wealthy feel thy blow,
    ·   From pomp and pleasure torn;
But oh! a blest relief for those
    That weary-laden mourn.
    'Man was Made to Mourn – A Dirge'

Can it be possible, that when I resign this frail, feverish
being, I shall still find myself in conscious existence!
When the last gasp of agony has announced that I am no
more to those that knew me, and the few who loved me;
when the cold, stiffened, unconscious, ghastly corse is
resigned into the earth, to be the prey of unsightly
reptiles, and to become in time a trodden clod, shall I yet
be warm in life, seeing and seen, enjoying and enjoyed?
Ye Sages and holy Flamens, is there probability in your
many conjectures, any truth in your many stories of
another world beyond death; or are they all alike
baseless visions and fabricated fables? If there is another
life, it must be only for the just, the benevolent, the
amiable, and the humane; what a flattering idea, then, is
a World to come! Would to God I as firmly believed it,
as I ardently wish it!
    to Mrs Dunlop, 13 December 1789

Well, madam, have you any commands for the other
world?

>to Maria Riddell, 5 July 1796
>Maria Riddell's *Memoir*

Devil

>O thou, whatever title suit thee!
>Auld Hornie, Satan, Nick, or Clootie,
>Wha in yon cavern grim an' sooty
>>Clos'd under hatches,
>Spairgies about the brunstane cootie,
>>To scaud poor wretches!

>Hear me auld Hangie, for a wee ...

>An' now, auld Cloots, I ken ye're thinkan
>A certain bardie's rantin, drinkin,
>Some luckless hour will send him linkan,
>>To your black pit;
>But faith! he'll turn a corner jinkan,
>>An' cheat you yet.
>'Address to the Deil'

I have bought a pocket Milton, which I carry perpetually
about with me, in order to study the sentiments –
the dauntless magnanimity; the intrepid unyielding
independence; the desperate daring, and noble defiance
of hardship, in that great personage, Satan.

>to William Nicol, 18 June 1787

>The Deil he couldna scaith thee,
>>Or aught that wad belang thee;
>He'd look into thy bonnie face
>>And say, 'I canna wrang thee!'
>'Bonnie Lesley'

In Se'enteen Hunder'n Forty-Nine
The Deil gat stuff to mak a swine,
    An' coost it in a corner;
But wilily he chang'd his plan,
An' shaped it something like a man,
    An' ca'd it Andrew Turner.
'On Andrew Turner'

The Devil got notice that Grose was a-dying,
So whip! at the summons, old Satan came flying;
But when he approach'd where poor Francis lay
      moaning,
And saw each bed-post with its burden a-groaning,
Astonished! confounded! cry'd Satan, by God,
I'll want 'im, ere I take such a damnable load.
  'Epitaph on Captain Francis Grose, the
  Celebrated Antiquary'

The deil cam fiddlin thro' the town,
    And danc'd awa wi' the Exciseman,
And ilka wife cries: 'Auld Mahoun,
    I wish you luck o' the prize, man!
  'The Deil cam Fiddlin thro' the Town'

Dear –, I'll gie ye some advice,
    You'll tak it no uncivil;
You shouldna paint at angels, man,
    But try and paint the devil.

To paint an angel's kittle wark,
    Wi' Nick, there's little danger
You'll easy draw a lang-kent face,
    But no sae weel a stranger.
  'Epigram Addressed to an Artist whom the Poet found
        Engaged on a Representation of Jacob's
        Dream'

Them that curst carmagole, auld Satan,
Watches like baudrons wi' a rattan
Our sinfu' saul to get a claut on,
    Wi' felon ire;
Syne, whip! his tail ye'll ne'er cast saut on,
    He's aff like fire.

Ah Nick! ah Nick! it is na fair,
First showing us the tempting ware,
Bright wines, and bonie lasses rare,
    To put us daft;
Syne weave unseen, thy spider snare
    O' hell's damned waft.
    'Epistle to Colonel Peyster'

I have a sore warfare in this world – the devil, the world, and the flesh are three formidable foes. The first, I generally try to fly from; the second, alas! generally flies from me; but the third is my plague, worse than the ten plagues of Egypt.
    to William Nicol, early March 1788

Though I am not without my fears respecting my fate, at the grand, universal inquest of the right and wrong commonly called *The Last Day*, yet I trust there is one sin which that archvagabond, Satan, who I understand is to be King's evidence, cannot throw in my teeth, I mean ingratitude.
    to John M'Auley, 4 June 1789

Disappointment

I have been all my life ... one of the rueful-looking, long-visaged sons of Disappointment. A damned Star has always kept my zenith, and shed its baleful influence ... I rarely hit where I aim; and if I want anything, I am almost sure never to find anything where I seek it.

to John Arnot, April 1787

I am tired with and disgusted at the language of complaint against the evils of life. Human existence in the most favourable situations does not abound with pleasures, and has its inconveniences and ills: capricious, foolish Man mistakes these inconveniences and ills as if they were the peculiar property of his particular situation; and hence that eternal fickleness, that love of change which has ruined and daily does ruin, many a fine fellow as well as many a Blockhead; and is almost without exception a constant source of disappointment and misery.

to Robert Ainslie, November 1789

Drama

We have gotten a set of very decent Players here just now. I have seen them an evening or two.

to Gilbert Burns, 11 January 1790

Our theatrical company ... leave us in a week. Their merit and character are indeed very great ... not a worthless creature among them; and their encouragement has been accordingly. Their usual run is from eighteen to twenty-five pounds a night: seldom less than the one, and the house will hold no more than the other. There have been repeated instances of sending away six, and eight, and ten pounds a night for want of room. A new theatre is to be built by subscription; the first stone is to be laid on Friday first to come. Three hundred guineas have been raised by thirty subscribers, and thirty more might have been got if wanted. The manager, Mr Sutherland, was introduced to me by a friend from Ayr;

and a worthier or cleverer fellow I have rarely met with. Some of our clergy have slipt in by stealth now and then ...
    to William Nicol, 9 February 1790

I have done little in the poetic way. I have given Mr Sutherland two Prologues, one of which was delivered last week.
    to William Nicol, 9 February 1790

I have got Shakespeare, and begun with him; and I shall ... make myself master of all the Dramatic Authors of any repute, in both English and French, the only languages which I know.
    to Lady Elizabeth Cunningham, 23 December 1789

Drink

Leeze me on Drink! it gies us mair
    Than either School or College;
It kindles Wit, it waukens Lear,
    It pangs us fou o' Knowledge.
Be't *whisky-gill* or *penny-wheep*,
    Or onie stronger potion,
It never fails, on drinkin deep
    To kittle up our *notion*,
        By night or day.
'The Holy Fair'

Long may we live! Long may we love!
    And long may we be happy!
And may we never want a glass
    Well charg'd with generous nappy!
'To Clarinda'

Fill me with a rosy wine,
Call a toast – a toast divine;
Give the Poet's darling flame,
Lovely Jessie be thy name;
Then thou mayest freely boast
Thou hast given a peerless toast.
   'On Jessie Lewars'

Go fetch to me a pint o' wine,
    And fill it in a silver tassie;
That I may drink, before I go,
    A service to my bonie lassie.
The boat rocks at the pier of Leith,
    Fu' loud the wind blaws frae the Ferry,
The ship rides by the Berwick-Law,
    An' I maun leave my bony Mary.
   'My Bony Mary'

Gane is the day, and mirk's the night,
But we'll ne'er stray for faute o' light;
Gude ale and brandy's stars and moon,
And blude-red wine's the risin sun.
    Then gudewife, count the lawin',
    The lawin', the lawin',
    Then gudewife, count the lawin',
    And bring a coggie mair.
   'Gudewife, Count the Lawin' '

O gude ale comes and gude ale goes,
    Gude ale gars me sell my hose,
Sell my hose and pawn my shoon,
    Gude ale keeps my heart aboon.
   'O Gude Ale Comes'

A man may drink and no be drunk.
  'There was a Lass, They Ca'd her Meg'

We are na fou, we're no that fou
But just a drappie in our ee.
  'Willie Brewed a Peck o' Maut'

Contented wi' little and cantie wi' mair.
When'er we forgather wi' Sorrow and Care,
I gie them a skelp, as they're creeping alang,
Wi' a cog o' gude swats and an auld Scottish sang.
  'A Coggie o' Yill'

Let other poets raise a fracas
'Bout vines, an' wines, an' druken *Bacchus*,
An' crabbed names an' stories wrack us,
    An' grate our lug,
I sing the juice *Scotch bear* can mak us,
    In glass or jug …

O thou, my Muse! guid, auld Scotch Drink!
Whether thro' wimplin worms thou jink,
Or, richly brown, ream owre the brink,
    In glorious faem,
Inspire me, till I lisp an' wink,
    To sing thy name! …

Leeze me on thee, John Barleycorn
    Thou king o' grain! …

Food fills the wame, an' keeps us livin':
Tho' life's a gift no worth receivin',
When heavy-dragg'd wi' pine an' grievin;
    But oil'd by thee,

The wheels o' life gae down-hill, scrievin'
    Wi' rattlin glee …

Thou clears the head o' doited Lear;
Thou cheers the heart o' drooping care;
Thou strings the nerves o' Labour-sair,
    At's weary toil;
Thou ev'n brightens dark despair,
    Wi' gloomy smile …

Wae worth that *Brandy*, burnan trash!
Fell source o' monie a pain an' brash!
Twins mony a poor, doylt, druken hash
    O' half his days;
An' sends, besides, auld Scotland's cash
    To her warst faes …

O whisky! soul o' plays an' pranks!
Accept a bardie's gratefu' thanks!
When wanting thee, what tuneless cranks
    Are my poor Verses!
  'Scotch Drink'

Inspiring bold John Barleycorn!
What dangers thou canst make us scorn!
Wi' tippeny, we fear nae evil;
Wi' usquebae, we'll face the devil!
  'Tam O' Shanter'

Then let us toast John Barleycorn,
  Each man a glass in hand;
And may his great posterity
    Ne'er fail in old Scotland!
  'John Barleycorn: A Ballad'

But tell me whisky's name in Greek.
  'The Author's Earnest Cry and Prayer'

There's some are fou o' love divine,
There's some are fou o' brandy.
  'The Holy Fair'

While we sit bowsing at the nappy,
An' getting fou and unco happy,
We thinkna on the lang Scots miles,
The mosses, waters, slaps and styles
That lie between us an' our hame,
Where sits our sultry, sullen dame,
Gathering her brows like gathering storm,
Nursing her wrath to keep it warm.
  'Tam O' Shanter'

I wasna fou, but just had plenty.
  'Death and Dr Hornbrook'

This I write to you when I am miserably fou,
consequently it must be the sentiments of my heart.
  to Peter Hill, 17 May 1787

You may guess that the convivial hours of *men* have
their mysteries of wit and mirth; and I hold it a piece of
contemptible baseness, to detail the sallies of thoughtless
merriment or the orgies of accidental intoxication, to the
ear of Sobriety or female Delicacy.
  to Mrs Dunlop, 5 February 1789

I am so completely nettled with the fumes of wine that I
cannot write anything like a letter.
  to Alexander Cunningham, Early autumn 1791

Care, mad to see a man sae happy,
E'en drown'd himsel amang the nappy.
As bees flee hame wi' lades o' treasure,
The minutes winged their way wi' pleasure;
Kings may be blest, but Tam was glorious,
O'er a' the ills o' life victorious …

Whene'er to drink you are inclin'd,
Or cutty sarks rin in your mind,
Think! ye may buy the joys o'er dear,
Remember Tam o' Shanter's mare.
   'Tam O' Shanter'

In honest Bacon's ingle-neuk,
   Here maun I sit and think;
Sick o' the warld and warld's fock,
   And sick, d-mned sick o' drink!…

Yestreen, alas! I was sae fu'
   I could but yisk and wink;
And now, this day, sair, sair I rue,
   The weary, weary drink.

Satan, I fear thy sooty claws,
   I hate thy brunstane stink,
And ay I curse the luckless cause,
   The wicked soup o' drink.

In vain I would forget my woes
   In idle rhyming clink,
For past redemption d-mned in Prose
   I can do nought but drink.
   'To William Stewart'

There's death in the cup – sae beware!
    Nay, more – there is danger in touching;
But wha can avoid the fell snare,
    The man and his wine's sae bewitching!
Inscription on a Goblet

Dullness

O Dulness, portion of the truly blest,
Calm, sheltered haven of eternal rest!
    'The Poet's Progress'

    Mammon's trusty cur
Clad in rich dulness' comfortable fur.
    'To Robert Graham of Fintry'

Education

Gie me ae spark o' Nature's fire,
That's a' the learning I desire.
    'First Epistle to John Lapraik'

What's a' your jargon o' your schools,
Your Latin names for horns and stools;
If honest Nature made you fools,
    What sairs your grammars?
    'First Epistle to John Lapraik'

English

The English steel we could disdain,
    Secure in valour's station;
But English gold has been our bane,
    Such a parcel of rogues in a nation …

But pith and power, till my last hour,
    I'll mak this declaration;
We're bought and sold for English gold,
    Such a parcel of rogues in a nation.
    'Such a Parcel of Rogues in a Nation'

Excise

To save me from that horrid situation of at any time going down, in a losing bargain of a farm, to misery, I have taken my Excise Instructions, and have my commission in my pocket for any emergency of fortune. If I could set *all* before your view, whatever disrespect you, in common with the world, have for this business, I know you would approve of my idea.

to Margaret Chalmers, 16 September 1788

My own farm here, I am pretty sure in time will do well; but for several years it will require assistance more than my pocket can afford. The Excise salary would pay half my rent, and I could manage the whole business of the Division without five guineas of additional expense.

to Lady Elizabeth Cunningham, 22 June 1789

I don't know if I have informed you that I am now appointed to an Excise Division, in the middle of which my house and farm lie ... I know how the word, Exciseman, or still more opprobrious, Gauger, will sound in your Ears. I, too, have seen the day when my auditory nerves would have felt very delicately on this subject, but a wife and children are things which have a wonderful power in blunting these kind of sensations! Fifty pounds a year for life, and provision for widows and orphans ... is no bad settlement for a poet.

to Robert Ainslie, 1 November 1789

The worst circumstance is, that the Excise Division which I have got is so extensive, no less than ten parishes to ride over; and it abounds, besides, with so much business that I can scarcely steal a spare moment. However, labour indears rest, and both together are absolutely necessary for the proper enjoyment of human existence.

to Richard Brown, 4 November 1789

I have been appointed to act in the capacity of Supervisor here, and I assure you, what with load of business, and what with that business being new to me, I could scarcely have commanded ten minutes to have spoken to you, had you been in town, much less to have written you an epistle. This appointment is only temporary and during the illness of the present incumbent; but I look forward to an early period when I shall be appointed in full form.

to Mrs Dunlop, 20 December 1794

I am giving up my farm; it is a bad bargain; and as my Landlord is offering the lands to sale, I took the hint, and have got some little consideration for my lease. The Excise, after all has been said against it, is the business for me. I find no difficulty in being an honest man in it; the work of itself is easy; and it is a devilish different affair, managing money matters when I care not a damn whether the money is paid or not; ... Beside, I am now ranked on the Supervisor list, which will in a little time, place me in a respectable situation, even as an Exciseman.

to Robert Cleghorn, October 1791

Now that the salary is £50 per ann. the Excise is surely a much superior object to a farm which, without some foreign assistance, must for half a lease be a losing bargain. The worst of it is, I know there are some respectable characters who do me the honour to interest themselves in my welfare and behaviour, and as leaving the farm so soon may have an unsteady, giddy-headed appearance, I had perhaps better lose a little money than hazard such people's esteem.

to Robert Graham, 31 July 1789

I have found the Excise business go on a great deal smoother with me than I apprehended ... I dare to be honest, and I fear no labour. Nor do I find my hurried life greatly inimical to my correspondence with the Muses. Their visits to me indeed ... like the visits of good angels, are short and far between; but I meet them now and then as I jog through the hills of Nithsdale.

to Robert Graham, 9 December 1789

People may talk as they please of the ignominy of the Excise, but what will support my family and keep me independent of the world is to me a very important matter; and I had much rather that my Profession borrowed credit from me, than that I borrowed credit from my Profession.

to Lady Elizabeth Cunningham, 23 December 1789

Searching auld wives' barrels,
    Ochon, the day!
That clarty barm should stain my laurels;
    But – what'll ye say!
These movin things ca'd wives and weans
Wad move the very heart o' stanes!
    'An Extemporaneous Effusion on being appointed to the
        Excise'

Five days in the week, or four at least, I must be on horseback, and very frequently ride thirty or forty miles ere I return; beside four different kinds of book-keeping to post every day.

to Mrs Dunlop, 2 October 1789

My fingers are so wore to the bone in holding the noses of his Majesty's liege subjects to the grindstone of Excise that I am totally unfit for wielding a pen in any generous subject.

to Dr James Anderson, 1 November 1790

I am going on, a mighty Tax-gatherer before the lord, and have lately had the interest to get myself ranked on the list of Excise as a Supervisor. I am not yet employed as such, but in a few years I will fall into the file of Supervisorship by seniority.

to Dr John Moore, 7 February 1791

I am now got ranked on the list as a Supervisor; and I have pretty good reason to believe that I shall soon be called out to employ. The appointment is worth from one to two hundred a year, according to the place of the country in which one is settled.

to Peter Hill, October 1791

Do not address to me Supervisor, for that is an honour I cannot pretend to: I am on the list, as we call it, for Supervisor, and will be called out by and by to act as one; but at present I am a simple gauger, tho' t'other day I got an appointment to an excise division of £25 per ann., better than the rest. My present income, down money is £70 per annum.

to Robert Ainslie, November 1791

Fame

I am in a fair way of becoming as eminent as Thomas à
Kempis or John Bunyan; and you may expect
henceforth to see my birthday inserted among the
wonderful events, in the Poor Robin's and Aberdeen
Almanacks, along with the black Monday, and the Battle
of Bothwell bridge.

to Gavin Hamilton, 7 December 1786

I leave Edinburgh in the course of ten days or a fortnight
… I have formed many intimacies and friendships here,
but I am afraid they are all of too tender a construction
to bear carriage a hundred and fifty miles. To the rich,
the great, the fashionable, the polite, I have no
equivalent to offer; and I am afraid my meteor
appearance will by no means entitle me to a settled
correspondence with any of you, who are the permanent
light of genius and literature.

to Dr John Moore, 23 April 1787

However the meteor-like novelty of my appearance in
the world might attract notice, and honour me with the
acquaintance of the permanent lights of genius and
literature … I knew very well that my utmost merit was
far unequal to the task of preserving that character when
once the novelty was over; I have made up my mind that
abuse, or almost even neglect, will not surprise me in my
quarters.

to Dr Hugh Blair, 3 May 1787

I have Philosophy or Pride enough to support me with
unwounded indifference against the neglect of my mere
dull Superiors, the merely rank and file of Noblesse and
Gentry; nay even to keep my vanity quite sober under
the larding of their Compliments; but from those who

are equally distinguished by their Rank and Character ...
their little notions and attentions are to me among the
first of earthly enjoyments.

to James M'Murdo, 26 November 1788

The partiality of my Countrymen has brought me
forward as a man of genius, and has given me a
Character to support. In the Poet, I have avowed manly
and independent sentiments, which I trust will be found
in the Man. Reasons of no less weight than the support
of a wife and children have pointed out as the elegible,
and indeed the only elegible line of life for me, my
present occupation. Still, my honest fame is my dearest
concern; and a thousand times have I trembled at the
idea of the degrading epithets that Malice, or
Misrepresentation may afix to my name. I have often, in
blasting anticipation, listened to some future hackney
Magazine Scribbler, with the heavy malice of savage
stupidity, exulting in his hireling paragraphs that 'Burns,
notwithstanding the fanfaronade of independence to be
found in his works, and after having been held forth to
Public View and Public Estimation as a man of some
genius, yet, quite destitute of resources within himself to
support this borrowed dignity, he dwindled into a paltry
Exciseman; and slunk out the rest of his existence in the
meanest of pursuits and among the vilest of mankind.' In
your illustrious hands, Sir, permit me to lodge my strong
disavowal and defiance of these slanderous falsehoods ...
I will indulge the flattering faith that my poetry will
considerably outlast my poverty.

to John Francis Erskine of Mar, 15 April 1793
(afterwards 27th Earl of Mar and 12th Lord Erskine)

Kings give coronets; alas, I can only bestow a ballad.
Still, however, I proudly claim one superiority even over
monarchs: my presents, so far as I am a poet, are the

presents of genius; and as the gift of R. Burns, they are the gifts of respectful gratitude to the worthy. I assure you, I am not a little flattered with the idea, when I anticipate children pointing out in future publications the tribute of respect I have bestowed on their mothers. The merits of the Scots airs, to which many of my songs are, and more will be, yet give me this pleasing hope.

    to John M'Murdo, July 1793

Family

To make a happy fireside clime
    To weans and wife,
That's the true pathos and sublime
    Of human life.
  'To Dr Blacklock'

Th' expectant wee things, toddlin', stacher through
    To meet their Dad, wi' flichterin' noise and glee.
His wee bit ingle, blinkin' bonnilie,
    His clean hearth-stane, his thrifty wifie's smile,
The lisping infant prattling on his knee,
    Does a' his weary kiaugh and care beguile,
An' makes him quite forget his labour and his toil.
  'The Cottar's Saturday Night'

Farming

Farming is also at a very low ebb with us. Our lands, generally speaking, are mountainous and barren; and our Landholders, full of ideas of farming gathered from the English, and the Lothians and other rich soils in Scotland; make no allowance for the odds of the quality of land, and consequently stretch us much beyond what, in the event, we will be found able to pay.

    to James Burness, 21 June 1783

Farming, the only thing of which I know anything, and heaven above knows but little do I understand of that ...
    to James Smith, 11 June 1787

When you kindly offered to accommodate me with a Farm, I was afraid to think of it, as I knew my circumstances unequal to the proposal; but now, when by the appearance of my second edition of my book, I may reckon on a middling farming capital, there is nothing I wish for more than to resume the Plough. Indolence and inattention to business I have sometimes been guilty of, but I thank my God, Dissipation and Extravagance have never been part of my character. If therefore, Sir, you could fix me in any sequester'd romantic spot, and let me have such a Lease as by care and industry I might live in humble decency, and have a spare hour now and then to write out an idle rhyme ... I am afraid, Sir, to dwell on the idea, lest Fortune have not such happiness in store for me ...
    to Patrick Miller, 1 May 1787

I want to be a farmer in a small farm, about a plough-gang, in a pleasant country, under the auspices of a good landlord. I have no foolish notion of being a Tenant on easier terms than another. To find a farm where one can live at all, is not easy. I only mean living soberly, like an old-style farmer, and joining personal industry.
    to Patrick Miller, 20 October 1787

I had intended to have closed my late meteorous appearance on the stage of Life, in the country Farmer; but after discharging some filial and fraternal claims, I find I could only fight for existence in that miserable manner, which I have lived to see throw a venerable

Parent in the jaws of jail; where, but for the Poor Man's last and often best friend, Death, he might have ended his days.

to Robert Graham, January 1788

I have at last ... entered in the list of Country farmers. I returned from Edinburgh on Saturday last, with my tack in my pocket; and since that time, I assure you, cares and business have occupied my every moment ... I have given up all literary correspondence, all conversation, all reading (prose reading) that is of the evaporating, dissipating kind ...

to Mrs Dunlop, 26 March 1788

I am so harassed with care and anxiety about this farming project of mine, that my Muse has degenerated into the veriest prose-wench that ever picked cinders, or followed a Tinker.

to Robert Cleghorn, 31 March 1788

Your Honourable Board, sometime ago gave me my Excise Commission, which I regard as my sheet-anchor in life. My farm, now that I have tried it a little, tho' I think it will in time be a saving bargain, yet does by no means promise to be such a pennyworth as I was taught to expect. It is in the last stage of worn-out poverty, and will take some time before it will pay the rent. I might have had the Cash to supply the deficiencies of these hungry years, but I have a younger brother and three sisters on a farm in Ayrshire; and it took all my surplus, over what I thought necessary for my farming capital, to save not only the comfort but the very existence of that fireside family circle from impending destruction. This was done before I took the farm; and rather than abstract my money from my brother, a circumstance which would ruin him, I will resign the farm and enter immediately into the service of your Honours.

to Robert Graham, 10 September 1788

In the first great concern of life, the means of supporting that life, I think myself tolerably secure. If my farm should not turn out well, which after all it may not, I have my Excise Commission in reserve. This last is comparatively a poor resource, but it is luxury to anything the first five and twenty years of my life taught me to expect.

to Lady Elizabeth Cunningham, 22 January 1789

My nerves are in a damnable State. I feel that horrid hypochondria pervading every atom of both body and soul. This Farm has undone my enjoyment of myself. But let it go to hell! I'll fight it out and be off with it.

to Gilbert Burns, 11 January 1790

My farm is a ruinous bargain, and would ruin me to abide by it. The Excise, notwithstanding all my objections to it, pleases me tolerably well; it is indeed my sole dependence. At Martinmas 1791, my rent rises to £20 per annum, and *then*, I am, on the maturest deliberation, determined to give it up; and still, even *then*, I shall think myself quite well quit, if I am no more than a hundred pounds out of Pocket. So much for Farming! Would to God I had never engaged in it. I can have in the Excise-line what they call a foot-walk whenever I choose; that is an appointment to a Division where I am under no necessity of keeping a horse.

to Mrs Dunlop, March 1790

Flowers

A rosebud by my early walk,
Adown a corn-enclosed bawk,
Sae gently bent its thorny stalk
    All on a dewy morning.

Ere twice the shades o' dawn are fled,
In a' its crimson glory spread,
And drooping rich the dewy head,
    It scents the early morning.
  'A Rosebud by My Early Walk'

Wee, modest, crimson-tippèd flow'r,
Thou'st met me in an evil hour;
For I maun crush amang the stoure
    Thy slender stem;
To spare thee now is past my pow'r,
    Thy bonie gem …

There, in thy scanty mantle clad,
Thy snawie bosom sun-ward spread,
Thou lifts thy unassuming head
    In humble guise;
But now the share uptears thy bed,
    And low thou lies!
  'To a Mountain Daisy, on turning one down with
        Plough in April'

Food

Some hae meat and canna eat,
And some wad eat that want it;
But we hae meat, and we can eat;
And sae the Lord be thank it.
  'The Selkirk Grace'

What though on hamely fare we dine,
    Wear hoddin grey, and a' that,
Gie fools their silks, and knaves their wine,
    A Man's a Man for a' that.
  'For a' That and a' That'

The halesome parritch, chief o' Scotia's food.
  'The Cottar's Saturday Night'

Fair fa' your honest, sonsie face
Great Chieftain o' the Puddin' race!
Aboon them a' ye tak your place,
    Painch, tripe, or thairm!
Weel are ye worthy o' a *grace*
    As lang's my arm.

The groaning trencher there ye fill,
Your hurdies like a distant hill,
Your *pin* wad help to mend a mill
    In time o' need,
While thro' your pores the dews distil
    Like amber bead …

Is there that owre his French *ragoût*,
Or *olio* wad staw a sow,
Or *fricassé* wad mak her spew
    Wi' perfect scunner,
Looks down wi' sneering, scornfu' view
    On sic a dinner? …

Ye Pow'rs wha mak mankind your care,
And dish them out their bill o' fare,
Auld Scotland wants nae stinking ware
    That jaups in luggies;
But, if ye wish her gratefu' prayer,
    Gie her a *Haggis*!
  'To a Haggis'

My blessings on ye, honest wife!
    I ne'er was here before;
Ye've wealth o' gear for spoon and knife –
    Heart could not wish for more.

Heav'n keep you clear o' sturt and strife,
    Till far ayont fourscore,
And while I toddle on thro' life,
    I'll ne'er gae by your door!
  'Epigram at Roslin Inn'

I ate some Newhaven broth, in other words, boiled mussels, with Mr Farquhar's family, t'other day.
    to Archibald Lawrie, 14 August 1787

You will certainly do me the honour to partake of a good Farmer's dinner with me. I shall promise you a piece of good old beef, a chicken, or perhaps a Nith salmon fresh from the ware, and a glass of good punch, on the shortest notice; and allow me to say, that Cincinnatus, or Fabricius, who presided in the august Roman Senate ... would have jumped at such a dinner.
    to Robert Graham, 13 May 1789

I lose my appetite at the sight of successful Knavery; sicken to loathing at the noise and nonsense of self-important Folly. When the hollow-hearted wretch takes me by the hand, the feeling spoils my dinner; the proud man's wine so offends my palate that it chokes me in the gullet; and the *pulvilis'd* feathered, pert coxcomb is so horrible in my nostril that my stomach turns. If ever you have any of these disagreeable sensations, let me prescribe for you Patience, and a bit of my Cheese ... Smellie ... too often is smarting at the pinch of distressful circumstances aggravated by the sneer of contumelious greatness – a bit of my cheese alone will not cure him, but if you add a tankard of Brown Stout and superadd a magnum of right Oporto, you will see his sorrows vanish like the morning mist before the summer sun.

to Peter Hill, 1 March 1791

By a carrier of yesterday ... I sent you a Kippered salmon, which I trust you will duly receive, and which I trust will give you many a toothful of satisfaction. If you have the confidence to say that there is anything of the kind in all your great city, superior to this in true kipper relish and flavour, I will be revenged by – not sending you another next season.

to Peter Hill, October 1794

I want you to dine with me today. I have two honest Midlothian Farmers with me, who have travelled three-score miles to renew old friendship with the Poet; and I promise you a pleasant party, a plateful of hotch-potch, and a bottle of good sound port.

to William Lorimer, August 1795

By the chaise, the driver of which brings you this, I send your *annual* Kipper; but on the express condition that you do not, like a fool as you were last year, put yourself to five times the value in expense of a return.

to Peter Hill, 19 January 1796

Fortune

Hail, thairm-inspirin, rattlin Willie!
Though Fortune's road be rough an' hilly
To ev'ry fiddling, rhyming billie,
    We never heed;
But tak it like th' unbacked fillie,
    Proud o' her speed ...

Hale be your heart! Hale be your fiddle
Lang may your elbuck jink and diddle
To cheer you through the wavy middle
    O' this vile warl:
Until ye on a cummock dridle,
    A gray-mired carl!
  'Epistle to Captain William Logan at Park'

Life's but a day at most,
Sprung from night, in darkness lost,
Hope not sunshine every hour,
Fear not, clouds will always lour.
  Written in Friar's Carse Hermitage: June, 1788 –
        Altered, December, 1788

Fortune has so much forsaken me, that she has taught
me to live without her; and amid my ragged poverty, I
am as independent, and much more happy than, a
monarch of the world.
  to Charles Sharpe, 22 April 1791

Freedom

Here's freedom to him that wad read,
Here's freedom to him that wad write!
There's nane ever feared that the truth should be
      heard,
But they whom the truth wad indite.
  'Here's a Health to Them that's Awa'

Scotland, my auld, respected Mither!
Tho' whiles ye moistify your leather,
Till when ye speak, ye aiblins blether;
    Yet deil-mak-matter!
Freedom and whisky gang thegither,
    Tak aff your whitter.
  'The Author's Earnest Cry and Prayer'

Heard ye o' the tree o' France,
    I watna what's the name o't;
Around it a' the patriots dance,
    Weel Europe kens the fame o't.
It stands where ance the Bastille stood,
    A prison built by kings, man,
When Superstition's hellish brood
    Kept France in leading strings, man.

Upo' this tree there grows sic fruit,
    Its virtues a' can tell, man;
It raises man aboon the brute,
    It maks him ken himsel, man.
Gif ance the peasant taste a bit,
    He's greater than a lord, man,
An' wi' the beggar shares a mite
    O' a' he can afford, man.
      'The Tree of Liberty' (attributed to Burns)

Free Masonry

I went to a Mason-lodge yesternight where the Most Worshipful Grand Master Charters, and all the Grand Lodge of Scotland visited. The meeting was most numerous and elegant; all the different Lodges about town were present, in all their pomp. The Grand Master who presided with great solemnity, and honour to himself as Gentleman and Mason, among other general toasts gave 'Caledonia and Caledonia's bard, brother Burns', which rung through the whole Assembly with multiplied honours and repeated acclamations. As I had no idea such a thing would happen, I was downright thunderstruck, and, trembling in every nerve, made the best return in my power. Just as I had finished, some of the Grand Officers said so loud as I could hear, with a

most comforting accent, 'Very well indeed!' which set
me something to rights again.
> to John Ballantine, 14 January 1787

May Freedom, Harmony, and Love,
    Unite you in the *grand Design*,
Beneath th' Omniscient Eye above –
    The glorious *Architect* Divine,
That you may keep th' *unerring line*,
    Still rising by the *plummet's law*
Till *Order* bright completely shine,
    Shall be my pray'r when far awa'.
> 'The Farewell, to the Brothers of St James's Lodge,
> Tarbolton'

Then fill up a bumper and make it o'erflow,
And honours masonic prepare for to throw;
May ev'ry true Brother of the Compass and Square
Have a big-bellied bottle when harassed with care.
> 'No Churchman am I'

Ye powers who preside o'er the wind and the tide,
    Who marked each element's border;
Who formed this frame with beneficient aim,
    Whose sovereign statute is Order;
Within this dear mansion may wayward contention
    Or withered envy ne'er enter;
May secrecy round be the mystical bound,
    And brotherly love be the centre.
> 'The Sons of Old Killie'

Friendship

Fate still has blest me with a friend,
    In ev'ry care and ill;
And oft a more endearing band,

A tie more tender still.
    It lightens, it brightens,
        The tenebrific scene,
    To meet with, and greet with,
        My Davie or my Jean.
'Epistle to Davie, a brother Poet'

Now if ye're ane o' warl's folk,
Wha rate the weaver by the cloak
An' sklent on poverty their joke
        Wi' bitter sneer,
Wi' you no friendship I will troke
        Nor cheap nor dear.
'To John Kennedy'

Here's a bottle and an honest friend!
    What wad ye wish for mair, man?
Wha kens, before his life may end,
    What his share may be of care, man.

Then catch the moments as they fly,
    And use them as ye ought, man:
Believe me, happiness is shy,
    And comes not ay when sought, man.
    Untitled

I have not a friend upon earth, besides yourself, to
whom I can talk nonsense without forfeiting some
degree of his esteem.
    to Robert Ainslie, 23 July 1787

I remember with pleasure, my dear Sir, a visit you talked
of paying to Dumfries, in Spring or Summer. I shall only
say I have never parted with a man, after so little
acquaintance, whom I more ardently wished to see
again.
    to David Blair, 23 January 1789

Every man has his virtues, and no man is without his failings; and curse on that privileged plain-dealing of friendship, which, in the hour of my calamity, cannot reach forth the helping hand, without at the same time, pointing out those failings, and assigning their share in my present distress.

> to Alexander Cunningham, 11 June 1791

Once fondly lov'd, and still remember'd dear,
    Sweet early object of my youthful vows,
Accept this mark of friendship, warm, sincere,
    Friendship! 'tis all cold duty now allows.
  'Lines to an Old Sweetheart'

Should auld acquaintance be forgot
    And never brought to mind?
Should auld acquaintance be forgot,
    And auld lang syne!

  For auld lang syne, my jo,
    For auld lang syne,
  We'll tak a cup o' kindness yet
    For auld lang syne....

And there's a hand, my trusty fiere!
    And gie's a hand o thine!
And we'll tak a right gude willie-waught,
    For auld lang syne.
  'For Auld Lang Syne'

Gardening

When rosy May comes in wi' flowers
To deck her gay, green-spreading bowers,
Then busy, busy are his hours,
    The gard'ner wi' his paidle.
  'The Gard'ner wi' his Paidle'

Ghosts

Ilk ghaist that haunts auld ha' or chamer,
Ye gypsy-gang that deal in glamour,
And you, deep-read in hell's black grammar,
    Warlocks and witches;
Ye'll quake at his conjuring hammer,
     Ye midnight bitches.
  'On the Late Captain Grose's Peregrinations through
      Scotland'

Let warlocks grim, an' wither'd hags,
Tell, how wi' you, on ragweed nags,
They swim the muirs and dizzy crags,
    Wi' wicked speed;
And in kirk-yairds renew their leagues,
    Owre howcket dead.
  'Address to the Devil'

Wow! Tam saw an unco sight!
Warlocks and witches in a dance;
Nae cotillion brent new frae France,
But hornpipes, jigs, strathspeys, and reels,
Put life and mettle in their heels.
A winnock-bunker in the east,
There sat auld Nick, in shape o' beast;
A towzie tyke, black, grim, and large,
To gie them music was his charge:
He screw'd the pipes and gart them skirl
Till roof and rafters a' did dirl.
  'Tam O' Shanter'

God

I am, I acknowledge, too frequently the sport of whim,
caprice, and passion, but reverence to God, and integrity
to my fellow creatures, I hope I shall ever preserve.
    to Sir John Whiteford, 1 December 1786

What Man could esteem, or what woman could love,
    Was He who lies under this sod;
If such Thou refusest admittance above,
    Then whom wilt thou favour, Good God!
  'Epitaph on R. Muir'

The heart benevolent and kind
    The most resembles God.
  'A Winter Night'

Greatness

To whom hae much, shall yet be given,
    Is every Great man's faith;
But he, the helpless, needful wretch
    Shall lose the mite he hath.
  'Extemporare – on some Commemorations of
      Thomson'

God knows I know very little of Great folks; and I hope
He can be my witness that for mere Greatness I as little
care. Worth, in whatever circumstances, I prize; but
worth conjoined with Greatness has a certain irresistible
power of attracting esteem.
  to John Ballantine, September 1786

Habits

Yours is the time of life for laying in habits; you cannot
avoid it, though you would choose, and these habits will
stick to your last sand. At after periods, even at so little
advance as my years, 'tis true, one may still be very
sharp-sighted to one's habitual failings and weaknesses,
but to eradicate or even amend them is quite a different
matter. Acquired at first, by accident, they by and by
begin to be, as it were, convenient; and in time are a
necessary part of our existence.
  to William Burns, 10 March 1789

Happiness

If you miss happiness by enjoyment, you will find it by contented resignation.

> to Thomas Orr, 17 November 1782

There is not a doubt but that health, talents, character, decent competency, respectable friends, are real and substantial blessings, and yet do we not daily see those who enjoy many or all these good things, and not withstanding, contrive to be as unhappy as others to whose lot few of them have fallen.

> to Alexander Cunningham, 14 February 1790

Health

Lord send you ay as weel's I want ye,
    And then ye'll do.
'Epistle to Dr Blacklock'

A lingering indisposition has hung about me for some time and has beaten me out of the use of pen and ink ...

> to William Nicol, 29 July 1787

Of late I have been confined with some lingering complaints originating, as I take it, in the stomach. To divert my spirits a little in this miserable fog of Ennui, I have taken a whim to give you a history of MYSELF.

> to Dr John Moore, 2 August 1787

I was ... unlucky in catching a miserable cold for which the medical gentlemen have ordered me into close confinement, 'under pain of Death!' the severest of penalties.

> to Patrick Miller, 20 October 1787

A certain sour-faced old acquaintance called Glauber's salts hinders me from my lesson tonight.

> to John Beugo, December 1787

Some weeks bypast indeed I have been a cripple in one of my legs, owing to a fall by the drunken stupidity of a coachman. I am got a good deal better, but can walk little yet without my crutches.

> to John Ballantine, January 1788

My curse on your envenom'd stang,
That shoots my tortur'd gums alang,
An'tho' my lugs gie mony a bang
    Wi' gnawin' vengeance,
Tearing my nerves wi' bitter twang,
    Like racking engines.

Whan fevers burn or agues seize us,
Rheumatics gnaw, or colics squeeze us,
Our neebour's sympathise, to ease us,
    Wi' pitying moan;
But thee – thou hell o' a' diseases –
    They mock our groan.

> 'Address to the Toothache'

For some nights ... I had slept in an apartment where the force of the winds and rains was only mitigated by being sifted through numberless apertures in the windows, walls, etc. In consequence, I was on Sunday, Monday, and part of Tuesday unable to stir out of bed, with all the miserable effects of a violent cold.

> to Mrs Dunlop, 28 April 1788

A bruised finger hindered me from transcribing my poem myself; so I am obliged to send you the inclosed, rather incorrect one.

> to John Ballantine, July 1788

The tremendous thunder-storm of yester-night and the lurid fogs of this morning have driven me, for refuge from the hypochondria which I fear worse than the devil, to my Muse.

> to Mrs Dunlop, 5 September 1788

I am scarce able to hold up my head with this fashionable influenza, which is just the rage now hereabouts.

> to Robert Graham, 23 September 1788

I know not of any particular cause for this worst of all my foes besetting me, but for some time my soul has been beclouded with a thickening atmosphere of evil imaginations and gloomy presages.

> to Mrs Dunlop, 21 June 1789

I have somehow got a most violent cold; and in the stupid, disagreeable predicament of a stuffed, aching head and an unsound, sickly crasis, do I sit down to thank you for yours of the nineteenth of October.

> to Mrs Dunlop, 8 November 1789

I am groaning under the miseries of a diseased nervous System; a System of all others the most essential to our happiness – or the most productive of our misery. For now near three weeks I have been so ill with a nervous headache, that I have been obliged to give up for a time my Excise-books, being scarce able to lift my head, much less to ride once a week over ten muir parishes.

> to Mrs Dunlop, 13 December 1789

I have had a bad tract of health most part of this winter … Thank Heaven, I am now got so much better as to be able to partake a little in the enjoyments of life.

> to William Dunbar, 14 January 1790

I have indeed been ill, Madam, the whole winter. An incessant headache, depression of spirits, and all the truly miserable consequences of a deranged nervous system, have made dreadful havoc of my health and peace. Add to all this, a line of life into which I have lately entered obliges me to ride, on the average, at least 200 miles every week. However, thank Heaven, I am now greatly better in my health.

 to Mrs Agnes M'Lehose, February 1790

A few days after I received yours I was seized with a slow, ill-formed fever, from which I am just risen out of the weary bed of sickness ... I have likewise had a most malignant squinancy which had me very near the precincts of the grave ... I am now got greatly better, though by no means in a confirmed state of health.

 to Alexander Dalziel, 5 October 1790

When I tell you, Madam, that by a fall, not from my horse but with my horse, I have been a cripple some time, and that this is the first day my arm and hand have been able to serve me in writing, you will allow that it is too good an apology for my seemingly ungrateful silence. I am now getting better, and am able to rhyme a little, which implies some tolerable ease; as I cannot think that the most poetic genius is able to compose on the rack.

 to Mrs Dunlop, 7 February 1791

Indigestion is the devil: nay, 'tis the devil and all. It besets a man in every one of his senses.

 to Peter Hill, March 1791

I was never more unfit for writing. A poor devil nailed to an elbow chair, writhing in anguish with a bruised leg, laid on a stool before him, is in a fine situation truly for saying bright things.

>   to Peter Hill, October 1791

As for myself, I am better, though not quite free from complaint. You must not think, as you seem to insinuate, that in my way of life I want exercise. Of that I have enough; but occasional hard drinking is the devil to me. Against this I have again and again bent my resolution, and have greatly succeeded. Taverns, I have totally abandoned; it is the private parties in the family way, among the hard-drinking gentlemen of this country, that does me the mischief – but even this, I have more than half given over.

>   to Mrs Dunlop, 2 January 1793

I am afraid that I am about to suffer for the follies of my youth. My medical friends threatened me with a flying gout, but I trust they are mistaken.

>   to Mrs Dunlop, 25 January 1794

You should have heard from me long ago; but, over and above some vexatious share in the pecuniary losses of these accursed times, I have, all this winter, been plagued with low spirits and blue devils, so that I have almost hung my harp upon the willow-trees.

>   to James Johnstone, February 1794

I am so poorly today as to be scarce able to hold my pen, and so deplorably stupid as to be totally unable to hold it to any purpose ... I know you are pretty deep read in Medical matters, but I fear you have nothing in the Materia Medica which can heal a diseased Spirit.

>   to Mrs Dunlop, September 1794

I am so ill as to be scarce able to hold this miserable pen
to this miserable paper.

> to Mrs Maria Riddell, Spring 1795

I had intended to have troubled you with a long letter;
but at present the delightful sensations of an omnipotent
Toothache so engross all my inner man, as to put it out
of my power even to write Nonsense ... Fifty troops of
infernal Spirits are riding post from ear to ear along my
jaw-bones.

> to William Creech, 30 May 1795

The health you wished for me in your Morning's Card is
I think, flown from me forever. I have not been able to
leave my bed today, till about an hour ago.

> to Mrs Maria Riddell, June or July 1795

Since I saw you, I have been much the child of disaster.
Scarcely begun to recover the loss of an only daughter
and darling child, I became myself the victim of a
rheumatic fever, which brought me to the borders of the
grave. After many weeks of sick-bed, I am just
beginning to crawl about.

> to Robert Cleghorn, January 1796

What sin of ignorance I have commited against so highly
valued a friend I am utterly at a loss to guess ... Will you
be so obliging, dear Madam, as to condescend on that
my offence which you seem determined to punish with a
deprivation of that friendship which was once the source
of my highest enjoyments? Alas! Madam, ill can I afford,
at this time, to be deprived of any of the small remnant
of my pleasures. I have lately drunk deep of the cup of
affliction. The Autumn robbed me of my only daughter
and darling child, and that at a distance too and so

rapidly as to put it out of my power to pay the last duties to her. I had scarcely begun to recover from that shock, when I became myself the victim of a most severe Rheumatic fever, and long the die spun doubtful; until after many weeks of a sick-bed it seems to have turned up more life, and I am beginning to crawl across the room, and once indeed have been before my own door in the street.

> to Mrs Dunlop, 31 January 1796

Alas! my dear Thomson, I fear it will be some time ere I tune my lyre again! ... Almost ever since I wrote you last, I have only known Existence by the pressure of the heavy hand of Sickness; and have counted time by the repercussions of Pain! Rheumatism, Cold and Fever have formed, to me, a terrible Trinity in unity, which makes me close my eyes in misery, and open them without hope.

> to George Thomson, April 1796

Still, still the victim of affliction: were you to see the emaciated figure who now holds the pen to you, you would not know your old friend ... Alas, Clarke, I begin to fear the worst!

> to James Clarke, 26 June 1796

My health being so precarious, nay dangerously situated, that as a last effort I am here at a sea-bathing quarters. Besides my inveterate rheumatism, my appetite is quite gone, and I am so emaciated as to be scarce able to support myself on my own legs.

> to George Thomson, 4 July 1796

It will be no very pleasing news to you that I am dangerously ill, and not likely to get better.

> to Gilbert Burns, 10 July 1796

Do, for heaven's sake, send Mrs Armour here immediately. My wife is hourly expecting to be put to bed. Good God! what a situation for her to be in, poor girl, without a friend! I returned from sea-bathing quarters today, and my medical friends would almost persuade me that I am better; but I think and feel that my strength is so gone that the disorder will prove fatal to me.

> to James Armour, 18 July 1796

Heaven

Here lies Boghead amang the dead,
    In hopes to get salvation;
But if such as he in Heav'n may be,
    Then welcome – hail! damnation.
    'Epitaph on James Grieve, Laird of Boghead, Tarbolton'

If there's another world, he lives in bliss;
If there is none, he made the best of this.
    'Epitaph on William Muir in Tarbolton Mill'

Highlands

When death's dark stream I ferry o'er,
    A time that surely shall come;
In Heaven itself, I'll ask no more,
    Than just a Highland welcome.
    A verse composed and repeated by Burns to the master
        of the house, on taking leave at a place in the
        Highlands, where he had been hospitably
        entertained.

My heart's in the Highlands, my heart is not here;
My heart's in the Highlands a-chasing the deer;
Chasing the wild deer, and following the roe,
My heart's in the Highlands wherever I go.

Farewell to the Highlands, farewell to the
      North;
The birthplace of valour, the country of worth;
Wherever I wander, wherever I rove,
The hills of the Highlands for ever I love.
   'My Heart's in the Highlands'

Himself

There was a lad was born in Kyle,
But whatna day o' whatna style,
I doubt it's hardly worth the while
    To be sae nice wi' Robin.

    Robin was a rovin' boy
      Rantin', rovin', rantin', rovin',
    Robin was a rovin' boy,
      Rantin', rovin', Robin!

Our monarch's hindmost year but ane
Was five an' twenty days begun,
'Twas then a blast o' Januar' win',
   Blew hansel in on Robin …

He'll hae misfortunes great an' sma',
But ay a heart aboon them a',
He'll be a credit till us a'
    We'll a' be proud o' Robin.
   'Rantin', Rovin', Robin'

I seem to be one sent into the world, to see, and observe;
and very easily compound with the knave who tricks me
of my money.
     to John Murdoch, 15 January 1783

Just now I've taen the fit o' rhyme,
My barmie noddle's working prime ...
   'Epistle to James Smith'

My father was a farmer upon the Carrick border,
And carefully he bred me in decency and order;
He bade me act a manly part, though I had ne'er a
      farthing;
For without an honest manly heart, no man was
      worth regarding.
   'My Father was a Farmer'

Ev'n then a wish (I mind its power)
A wish, that to my latest hour
    Shall strongly heave my breast;
That I for poor auld Scotland's sake
Some useful plan, or book could make,
    Or sing a song at least.
   'The Answer' (to the Guidwife of Wauchope House)

This while my notion's taen a sklent
To try my fate in guid, black prent;
But still the mair I'm that way bent,
    Something cries 'Hoolie!
I red you, honest man, tak tent!
    Ye'll shaw your folly.

There's ither poets much your betters,
Far seen in Greek, deep men o' letters,
Hae thought they had ensur'd their debtors,
    A' future ages;
Now moths deform, in shapeless tatters,
    Their unknown pages.'
   'Epistle to James Smith'

O life! Thou art a galling load,
Along a rough and weary road,
     To wretches such as I!
  'Despondency, an Ode'

An anxious e'e I never throws
Behint my lug, or by my nose;
I jouk beneath Misfortune's blows
     As weel's I may;
Sworn for to sorrow, care and prose,
     I rhyme away.
  'Epistle to James Smith'

Is there a man whose judgement clear
Can others teach the course to steer
Yet runs, himself, life's mad career,
     Wild as the wave?
Here, pause – and thro' the starting tear,
     Survey his grave.

The poor inhabitant below
Was quick to learn and wise to know,
And keenly felt the friendly glow,
     And softer flame;
But thoughtless follies laid him low,
     And stained his name!
  'A Bard's Epitaph'

Lord help me thro' this warld o' care!
I'm weary sick o't late and air!
Not but I hae a richer share
     Than mony others;
But why should ae man better fare
     And a' men brithers?
  'Epistle to Dr Blacklock'

I am nae poet, in a sense;
But just a rhymer like by chance.
An' hae to learning nae pretence;
    Yet, what's the matter,
Whene'er my Muse does on me glance,
    I jingle at her.
  'Epistle to J. Lapraik'

Some rhyme a neebor's name to lash;
Some rhyme (vain thought) for needfu' cash;
Some rhyme to court the contra clash,
    An' raise a din;
For me, an aim I never fash;
    I rhyme for fun …

The star that rules my luckless lot,
Has fated me the russet coat,
An' damned by fortune to the groat;
    But, in requit,
Has blest me with a random shot
    O' countra wit.
  'Epistle to James Smith'

The mair they talk I'm kent the better.
    E'en let them clash.
  'E'en Let Them Clash'

Leeze me on rhyme! it's ay a treasure,
My chief, amaist my only pleasure,
At hame, a-fiel, at work or leisure,
    The Muse, poor Lizzie!
Tho' rough and raploch be her measure,
    She's seldom lazy.
  'Second Epistle to Davie'

The bridegroom may forget the bride
 Was made his wedded wife yestreen;
The monarch may forget his crown
 That on his head an hour has been;
The mother may forget the child
 That smiles sae sweetly on her knee;
But I'll remember thee, Glencairn,
 And a' that thou hast done for me!
 'Lament for James, Earl of Glencairn'

Here, for my wonted rhyming raptures,
I sit and count my sins by chapters;
For life and spunk like ither Christians,
I'm dwindled down to mere existence,
Wi' nae converse but Gallowa' bodies,
Wi' nae kend face but Jenny Geddes.
 'Epistle to Hugh Parker'

All in this mottie, misty clime,
I backward mus'd on wasted time,
How I had spent my youthfu' prime,
 An' done nae-thing,
But stringing blethers up in rhyme
 For fools to sing.

Had I to guid advice but harket,
I might, by this, hae led a market,
Or strutted in a bank and clarket
 My cash account;
While here, half-mad, half-fed, half-sarket,
 Is a' the amount.
 'The Vision: First Duan'

God knows, I'm no the thing I should be,
Nor am I even the thing I cou'd be,

But twenty times, I rather wou'd be
    An atheist clean,
Than under gospel colours hid be
    Just for a screen.
    to the Reverend John McMath, enclosing a copy of *Holy Willie's Prayer* which he had requested.

Misfortune dogs the path of human life; the poetic mind finds itself miserably deranged in, and unfit for the walks of business; add to all, that, thoughtless follies and harebrained whims, like so many Ignes fatui, eternally diverging from the right line of sober discretion, sparkle with step-bewitching blaze in the idle-gazing eyes of the poor Bard, till, pop, 'he falls like Lucifer, never to hope again'. God grant that this may be an unreal picture with respect to me! but should it not, I have very little dependence on Mankind.
    to William Nicol, 18 June 1787

I generally like pretty well to hear myself speak.
    to George Reid, 19 April 1787

I am ill-skilled in beating the coverts of imagination for metaphors of gratitude.
    to Dr John Moore, 23 April 1787

There are just two creatures I would envy; a horse in his native state traversing the forests of Asia, or an oyster on some of the desert shores of Europe. The one has not a wish without enjoyment, the other has neither wish nor fear.
    to Margaret Chalmers, 19 December 1787

But I am an odd being; some yet unnamed feelings; things, not principles, but better than whims, carry me farther than boasted reason ever did a Philosopher.
    to Mrs M'Lehose, 8 December 1787

If I were in the [Excise] Service, it would ... favour my poetical schemes. I am thinking of something in the rural way of the Drama-kind. Originality of character is, I think, the most striking beauty in that species of composition, and my wanderings in the way of my business would be vastly favourable to my picking up original traits of Human nature.

to Robert Graham, 10 September 1788

Men are said to flatter women because they are weak; if it is so, Poets must be weaker still; for Misses Rachel and Keith, and Miss Georgina McKay, with their flattering attentions and artful compliments, absolutely turned my head. I own they did not lard me over as a Poet does his Patron or still more his Patroness, nor did they sugar me as a Cameronian Preacher does Jesus Christ; but they so intoxicated me with their sly insinuations and delicato innuendoes of Compliment that if it had not been for a lucky recollection how much additional weight and lustre your good opinion and friendship must give me in that circle, I had certainly looked on myself as a person of no small consequence.

to Mrs Dunlop, 13 November 1788

The heart of the Man and the fancy of the Poet are the two grand considerations for which I live.

to Mrs Dunlop, 7 December 1788

I have such a host of Peccadillos, Failings, Follies and Backslidings (anybody but myself might perhaps give some of them a worse appellation) that by way of some balance, however trifling, in the account, I am fain, so far as my very limited power reaches, to do any good I can to my fellow-creatures, merely for the selfish purpose of clearing a little the vista of Retrospection.

to the Reverend George H. Baird, 28 February 1791

From the manner in which God has divided the good things of this life, it is evident that He meant one part of Mankind to be the Benefactors and the other to be the Benefacted; and as he has thrown me among this latter Class, I would wish to acquiesce with cheerfulness.

to Mrs Dunlop, 8 July 1789

The truth is, that I am the most indolent of all human beings; and when I matriculate in the Herald's office, I intend that my supporters shall be two sloths, my crest a slow-worm, and motto, 'Deil tak the foremost'.

to an unidentified correspondent, 1791?

I do not want to be independent, that I may sin; but I want to be independent in my sinning.

to Alexander Cunningham, 11 June 1791

Sunday closes a period of our cursed revenue business, and may probably keep me employed with my pen until Noon. Fine employment for a Poet's pen! There is a species of the Human genus that I call the Gin-Horse class; what enviable dogs they are! Round, and round, and round they go ... without an idea or wish beyond their circle; fat, sleek, stupid, patient, quiet and contented; while here I sit, altogether Novemberish, a damned mélange of Fretfulness and melancholy; not enough of the one to rouse me to passion, nor of the other to repose me in torpor; my soul flouncing and fluttering round her tenement, like a wild Finch caught amid the horrors of winter and newly thrust in a cage.

to Mrs Maria Riddell, November 1793

The honest heart that's free frae a'
    Intended fraud or guile,
However fortune nick the ba'
    Has ay some cause to smile.
'Epistle to Davie, a Brother Poet'

Jacobin

I was in the playhouse one night, when Ça Ira was called for. I was in the middle of the Pit, and from the Pit the clamour arose. One or two individuals with whom I occasionally associate were of the party, but I neither knew of the Plot, nor joined in the plot; nor even opened my lips to hiss, or huzza, that, or any other Political tune whatever. I looked on myself as far too obscure a man to have any weight in quelling a Riot; at the same time as a character of higher respectability, than to yell in the howlings of a rabble. This was the conduct of all the first Characters in this place; and these Characters know, and will avow, that such was my conduct. I never uttered any invectives against the king. His private worth, it is altogether impossible that such a man as I, can appreciate; and in his Public capacity, I always revered, and ever will, with the soundest loyalty, revere, the Monarch of Great Britain as, to speak in Masonic, the sacred Keystone of our Royal Arch Constitution.

As to Reform Principles, I look upon the British Constitution, as settled at the Revolution, to be the most glorious Constitution on earth, or that perhaps the wit of man can frame; at the same time, I think, and you know what High and distinguished Characters have for some time thought so, that we have a good deal deviated from the original principles of that Constitution, particularly, that an alarming System of Corruption has pervaded the connection between the Executive Power and the House of Commons. This is the Truth, the Whole truth, of my Reform opinions; opinions which, before I was aware of the complexion of these innovating times, I too unguardedly (now I see it) sported with: but henceforth, I seal my lips …

As to France, I was her enthusiastic votary in the beginning of the business. When she came to show her

old avidity for conquest, in annexing Savoy etc., to her
dominions, and including the rights of Holland, I altered
my sentiments.

> to Robert Graham, 5 January 1793

Jacobitism

Perdition, baleful child of night!
Rise and revenge the injured right
  Of Stuart's royal race;
Lead on the unmuzzled hounds of hell,
Till all the frighted echoes tell
  The blood-notes of the chase;
Full on the quarry point their view,
Full on the base, usurping crew,
The tools of faction and the nation's curse.
'Birthday Ode for 31 December, 1787'

Whare hae ye been sae braw, lad!
  Whare hae ye been sae brankie O?
Whare hae ye been sae braw, lad?
  Cam ye by Killiecrankie O?

An ye had been whare I hae been,
  Ye wadna been sae cantie O,
And ye had seen what I hae seen,
  I' the braes o' Killiecrankie O.
'Killiecrankie'

Come boat me o'er, come row me o'er,
  Come boat me o'er to Charlie;
I'll gie John Ross anither bawbee
  To boat me o'er to Charlie.

We'll o'er the water, we'll o'er the sea,
  We'll o'er the water to Charlie;

Come weal, come woe, we'll gather and go,
    And live or die wi' Charlie.
  'O'er the Water to Charlie'

Awa whigs awa,
    Awa whigs awa,
Ye're but a pack o' traitor louns,
    Ye'll do nae gude at a'.

Our thrissles flourish'd fresh and fair,
    And bonie bloom'd our roses;
But whigs cam, like a frost in June,
    And wither'd a' our posies.

Our ancient crown's fa'n in the dust;
    Deil blin' them wi' the stoure o't,
And write their names in his black beuk
    Wha gae the whigs the power o't! …

Grim Vengeance lang has taen a nap,
    But we may see him wauken:
Gude help the day when royal heads
    Are hunted like a maukin.
  'Awa Whigs Awa'

Carl an the king come,
Carl an the king come;
Thou shalt dance and I will sing,
Carl an the king come.

An somebodie were come again,
Then somebodie maun cross the main,
And everyman shall hae his ain,
Carl an the king come.
  'Carl an the King Come'

My love was born in Aberdeen,
The boniest lad that e'er was seen,
But now he makes our hearts fu' sad,
He takes the field wi' his white cockade.

O he's a ranting, roving lad,
He is a brisk and bonny lad,
Betide what may, I will be wed,
And follow the boy wi' the white Cockade.
   'The White Cockade'

It was a' for our rightfu' king
    We left fair Scotland's strand;
It was a' for our rightfu' king
    We e'er saw Irish land, my dear,
    We e'er saw Irish land.
   'It was a' for our Rightfu' King'

The injured Stuart line is gone,
A race outlandish fills their throne;
An idiot race, to honour lost;
Who know them best, despise them most.
   'Written by Somebody On The Window of an Inn at
         Stirling, on Seeing the Royal Palace in Ruin'

'Twas on a Monday morning,
    Right early in the year,
That Charlie cam to our town,
    The young Chevalier.

An' Charlie he's my darling, my darling, my darling,
Charlie he's my darling, the young Chevalier.
   'Charlie He's My Darling'

Sir John Cope trode the north right far,
Yet ne'er a rebel he cam naur,
Until he landed at Dunbar
Right early in the morning.
>   Hey Johnie Cope are ye waukin yet,
>   Or are ye sleeping I would wit?
>   O haste ye get up for the drums do beat,
>   O fye Cope rise in the morning.

He wrote a challenge from Dunbar,
Come fight me Charlie an ye daur;
If it be not by the chance of war,
I'll give you a merry morning.

When Charlie look'd the letter upon
He drew his sword the scabbard from –
'So heaven restore me to my own,
I'll meet, you, Cope, in the morning' ...

But when he saw the Highland lads
Wi' tartan trews and white cockauds,
Wi' swords and guns and rungs and gauds,
O Johnie he took wing in the morning ...

Sir Johnie into Berwick rade,
Just as the devil had been his guide;
Gien him the warld he wouldna stay'd,
To foughten the boys in the morning.

Say the Berwickers unto Sir John,
O what's become of all your men?
In faith, says he, I dinna ken,
I left them a' this morning ...
>   'Johnie Cope'

Here's a health to them that's awa',
Here's a health to them that's awa'.
Here's a health to Charlie, the chief o' the clan,
Although that his band be but sma'.
  'Here's a Health to Them that's Awa'

Satan sits in his black neuk,
    My bonie laddie, Highland laddie,
Breaking sticks to roast the Duke,
    My bonie laddie, Highland laddie.
The bloody monster gae a yell,
    My bonie laddie, Highland laddie,
And loud the laugh gaed round a' hell,
    My bonie laddie, Highland laddie.
  'I hae been at Crookieden'

I went last Wednesday to my parish church, most
cordially to join in grateful acknowledgements to the
Author of all Good, for the consequent blessings of the
Glorious Revolution ... Bred and educated in revolution
principles, the principles of reason and common sense, it
could not be any political prejudice that made my heart
revolt at the harsh abusive manner in which the
Reverend Gentleman mentioned the House of Stuart ...
We may rejoice sufficiently in our deliverance from past
evils, without cruelly raking up the ashes of those whose
misfortune it was, perhaps, as much as their crimes, to be
the authors of these evils ... cursing a few ruined
powerless exiles, who only harboured ideas and made
attempts, that most of us would have done, had we been
in their situation.
    to the Editor of the *Edinburgh Evening Courant*,
    8 November 1788

Kissing

Humid seal of soft affections,
    Tenderest pledge of future bliss,
Dearest tie of young connections,
    Love's first snowdrop, virgin bliss!
  'To a Kiss'

Lallans

In days when mankind were but callans
At grammar, logic, an' sic talents,
They took nae pains their speech to balance,
    Or rules to gie:
But spak their thochts in plain, braid Lallans,
    Like you or me.
  'Epistle to William Simson'

Law

He clench'd his pamphlets in his fist,
    He quoted and he hinted,
Till, in a declamation mist,
    His argument he tint it:
He gap'd for it, he grap'd for't,
    He fand it was awa, man;
But what his common sense came short,
    He ekèd out wi' law, man.
  'Lord Advocate', Epigrams, Extemporare in the Court
        of Session'

When neighbours anger at a plea,
An' just as wud as wud can be,
How easy can the *barley-bree*
    Cement the quarrel.
It's aye the cheapest lawyer's fee,
    To taste the barrel.
  'Scotch Drink'

I do not know if passing a 'Writer to the Signet' be a trial of scientific merit or a mere business of friends and interests ... I grant you enter the lists of life, to struggle for bread, business, notice, and distinction, in common with hundreds. But who are they? Men like yourself, and of that aggregate body, your compeers, seven-tenths of them come short of your advantages natural and accidental; while two of those that remain, either neglect their parts, as flowers blooming in the desert, or misspend their strength, like a bull goring a bramble bush.

to Robert Ainslie, 6 January 1789

Liberty

Be Britain still to Britain true,
    Amang ourselves united;
But never but by British hands
    Maun British wrangs be righted.
'Does Haughty Gaul Invasion Threat'

Who will not sing 'God save the King'
    Shall hang as high's the steeple;
But while we sing 'God save the King',
    We'll ne'er forget THE PEOPLE!
'Does Haughty Gaul Invasion Threat'

A fig for those by law protected!
    LIBERTY'S a glorious feast!
Courts for Cowards were erected,
    Churches built to please the Priest.
'The Jolly Beggars'

Who wou'd to Liberty e'er prove disloyal,
May his son be a hangman, and he his first trial.
'A Toast'

Liberty's in every blow!
   Let us do or die!
  'Scots Wha Hae'

Life

O enviable early days,
When dancing thoughtless pleasure's maze,
   To care, to guilt unknown!
How ill exchang'd for riper times,
To feel the follies, or the crimes,
   Of others, or my own!
  'Despondency – An Ode'

Life is all a variorum
   We regard not how it goes.
Let them cant about decorum
   Who have character to lose.
  'The Jolly Beggars'

When ance life's day draws near the gloamin',
Then farewell vacant, careless roamin',
An' farewell cheerfu' tankards foamin',
   An' social noise;
An' farewell dear, deluding woman,
   The joy o' joys!
  'Epistle to James Smith'

Sometimes, indeed, when for an hour or two … my spirits are a little lightened, I glimmer a little into futurity; but my principal, and indeed my only pleasurable employment is looking backwards and forwards in a moral and religious way. I am quite transported at the thought that ere long, perhaps very soon, I shall bid an eternal adieu to all the pains, and uneasiness and disquietude of this weary life …
    to William Burns, 27 December 1781

Man is by no means a happy creature. I do not speak of
the selected few, favoured by partial Heaven; whose
souls are tuned to gladness and riches, and honours, and
prudence, and wisdom. I speak of the neglected many,
whose nerves, whose sinews, whose days, whose
thoughts, whose independence, whose peace, nay,
whose very gratifications and enjoyments, the instinctive
gifts of nature, are sacrificed and sold to these few
bloated minions of heaven!

    to Mrs Dunlop, 27 March 1788

Life is but a day at most,
Sprung from night, in darkness lost;
Hope not sunshine ev'ry hour,
Fear not clouds will always lour.
Happiness is but a name,
Make CONTENT and EASE thy aim.
Ambition is a meteor gleam,
Fame a restless airy dream;
Pleasures, insects on the wing
Round peace, the tenderest flower of spring;
Those that sip the dew alone,
Make the butterflies thy own;
Those that would the bloom devour,
Crush the locusts, save the flower.
For the FUTURE be prepar'd,
Guard, wherever thou canst guard,
But thy utmost duty done,
Welcome what canst not shun;
Follies past, give thou to air;
Make their consequence thy care:
Keep the name of MAN in mind,
And dishonour not thy kind.
Reverence with lowly heart
Him whose wondrous work thou art;

Keep his GOODNESS still in view,
Thy trust – and thy example too.
> Written in Friar's Carse Hermitage on the banks of Nith
> – June, 1788

Life is a fairy scene; almost all that deserves the name of enjoyment, or pleasure, is only a charming delusion and in comes ripening Age, in all the gravity of hoary wisdom, and wretchedly chases away the bewitching Phantom.
> to Captain Brown, 24 February 1788

I have a hundred times wished that one could resign life as an officer resigns a commission; for I would not *take in* any poor ignorant wretch, by *selling out*. Lately I was a sixpenny private, and, God knows, a miserable soldier enough; now I march to the campaign, a starving cadet: a little more conspicuously wretched … I am ashamed of all this; for though I do not want bravery for the warfare of life, I could wish, like some other soldiers, to have as much fortitude or cunning as to dissemble or conceal my cowardice.
> to Mrs Dunlop, 21 January 1788

What strange beings we are! Since we have a portion of conscious existence, equally capable of enjoying Pleasure, Happiness and Rapture, or of suffering Pain, Wretchedness and Misery, it is surely worthy of enquiry whether there be not such a thing as a Science of life; whether Method, Economy and Fertility of expedients, be not applicable to Enjoyment; and whether there be not a want of dexterity in Pleasure which renders our little scantling of happiness still less, and a profuseness, an intoxication of bliss, which leads to Satiety, Disgust and Self-abhorrence.

There is not a doubt but that health, talents, character, decent competency, respectable friends, are real and substantial blessings; and yet do we not daily see those who enjoy many or all of these good things, and notwithstanding, contrive to be as unhappy as others to whose lot few of them have fallen.

I believe one great source of this mistake or misconduct is owing to a certain stimulus with our Ambition, which goads us up the hill of life, not as we ascend other eminences, for the laudable curiosity of viewing an extended landscape, but rather for the dishonest pride of looking down on others of our fellow-creatures seemingly diminutive in humbler stations.

to Alexander Cunningham, written December 1789, sent 16 February 1790

Do you not think, Madam, that among the few favoured of Heaven in the structure of their minds ... there may be a purity, a tenderness, a dignity, an elegance of soul, which are of no use, nay in some degree, absolutely disqualifying, for the truly important business of making a man's way into life?

to Mrs Dunlop, 10 April 1790

What hidden trap-doors of disaster, what unseen arrows of misfortune, waylay and beset our path of life!

to Mrs Dunlop, 9 July 1790

I have not passed half the ordinary term of an old man's life, and yet I scarcely look over the obituary of a Newspaper that I do not see some names that I have known, and which I, and other acquaintances, little thought to meet with there so soon. Every other instance of the mortality of our kind, makes us cast a horrid anxious look into the dreadful abyss of uncertainty, and shudder with apprehension for our fate.

to Mrs Dunlop, 6 December 1792

What a transient business is life! Very lately I was a boy; but t'other day I was a young man; and I already begin to feel the rigid fibre and stiffening joints of Old Age coming fast o'er my frame. With all my follies of youth, and I fear, a few vices of manhood, still, I congratulate myself on having had in early days religion strongly impressed on my mind. I have nothing to say to anybody as to which Sect they belong, or what Creed they believe; but I look on the Man who is firmly persuaded of Infinite Wisdom and Goodness superintending and directing every circumstance that can happen in his lot I felicitate such a man as having a solid foundation for his mental enjoyment; a firm prop and sure stay, in the hour of difficulty, trouble and distress; and a never-failing anchor of hope, when he looks beyond the grave.

to Mrs Dunlop, 20 December 1794

A life of literary leisure, with a decent competence, is the summit of my wishes.

to Patrick Heron, March 1795

Love

Perhaps I ought to make a long Preface of apologies for the freedom I am going to take, but as my heart means no offence but on the contrary is rather too warmly interested in your favour, for that reason I hope you will forgive me when I tell you that I most sincerely and affectionately love you. I am a stranger in these matters A[lison], as I assure you, that you are the first woman to whom I ever made such a declaration so I declare I am at a loss how to proceed.

    to Alison Begbie, 1781

Except your company, there is nothing on earth gives me so much pleasure as writing to you, yet it never gives me those giddy raptures so much talked of among lovers. I have often thought that if a well-grounded affection be not really a part of virtue, 'tis something extremely akin to it.

    to Alison Begbie, 1781

The language of the heart is … the only courtship I shall ever use to you.

    to Alison Begbie, 1781

I do love you if possible better for having so fine a taste and turn for Poesy.

    to Mrs Agnes M'Lehose, 28 December 1787

Far beyond all the other impulses of my heart was, un penchant à l'adorable moitiée du genre humain. My heart was completely tinder, and was eternally lighted by some Goddess or other; like every warfare in this world, I was sometimes crowned with success, and sometimes mortified with defeat.

    to Dr John Moore, 2 August 1787

About the first, and fourth quarters of the moon, I generally set in for the trade-winds of wisdom; but about the full, and change, I am the luckless victim of mad tornadoes, which blow me into chaos. Almighty Love still 'reigns and revels' in my bosom; and I am at

this moment ready to hang myself for a young
Edinburgh widow, who was wit and beauty more
murderously fatal than the assassinating stiletto of the
Sicilian banditti, or the poisoned arrow of the savage
African.

to Captain Richard Brown, 30 December 1787

My heart is sair – I dare na tell,
    My heart is sair for somebody;
I could wake a winter night
    For the sake o' Somebody.
      O-hon! for Somebody.
      O-hon! for Somebody.
I cou'd range the warld around
    For the sake o' Somebody.
'For the Sake o' Somebody'

If Heaven a draught of heavenly pleasure spare –
One cordial in this melancholy vale,
'Tis when a youthful, loving, modest pair,
In other's arms breathe out the tender tale,
Beneath the milk-white thorn that scents the evening
    gale.
'The Cottar's Saturday Night'

Your falling in love is indeed a phenomenon ... I am,
you know, a veteran in these campaigns, so let me advise
you always to pay your particular assiduities and try for
intimacy as soon as you feel the first symptoms of the
passion.

to William Burns, 5 May 1789

Had we never lov'd sae kindly,
Had we never lov'd sae blindly,
Never met – or never parted,
We had ne'er been broken-hearted ...

But to see her was to love her,
Love but her, and love for ever.
  'Ae Fond Kiss'

Oh, what a fool I am in love! What an extravagant
prodigal of affection! Why are your sex called the tender
sex, when I never met with one who can repay me in
passion? They are either not so rich in love as I am, or
are niggards where I am lavish.
  to Mrs Agnes M'Lehose, 21 January 1788

Tho' poor in gear, we're rich in love.
  'The Soldier's Return'

The wisest man the warl' saw,
    He dearly lov'd the lassies O.
  'Green Grow the Rashes'

In my conscience I believe that my heart has been so oft
on fire that it is absolutely vitrified. I look on the sex
with something like the admiration with which I regard
the starry sky in a frosty December night.
  to Margaret Chalmers, October 1787

O, my love's like a red, red rose
    That's newly sprung in June;
O my love's like the melodie
    That's sweetly played in tune.
  'My Love is like a Red, Red Rose'

The cares o' Love are sweeter far
    Than onie other pleasure;
And if sae dear its sorrows are,
    Enjoyment, what a treasure!
  'The Cares O' Love'

The captive bands may chain the hands,
    But love enslaves the man.
  'Beware o' Bonnie Annie'

The sacred lowe o' weel-plac'd love,
    Luxuriantly indulge it;
But never tempt th' illicit rove
    Tho' naething should divulge it:
I wave the quantum o' the sin,
    The hazard of concealing;
But, och! it hardens a' within,
    And petrifies the feeling.
  'Epistle to a Young Friend'

Not withstanding everything that has been said against
Love, respecting the folly and weakness it leads a young
unexpected mind into; still I think it, in a great measure,
deserves the highest encomiums that have been passed
on it. If anything on earth deserves the name of rapture
or transport, it is the feelings of green eighteen in the
company of the mistress of his heart when she repays
him with an equal return of affection.
  First Commonplace Book, April 1783

For my own part I never had the least thought or
inclination of turning Poet till I got heartily in Love, and
then Rhyme and Song were, in a manner, the
spontaneous language of my heart.
  First Commonplace Book, August 1783

You know our country custom of coupling a man and a
woman together as Partners in the labours of the
Harvest. In my fifteenth autumn, my Partner was a
bewitching creature who just counted an autumn less …
She was a bonie, sweet, sonsie lass. In short, she

altogether unwittingly to herself, initiated me in a certain delicious Passion, which in spite of acid Disappointment, gin-horse Prudence and book-worm Philosophy, I hold to be the first of human joys, our dearest pleasure here below ... Among her other love-inspiring qualifications, she sung sweetly; and 'twas her favourite reel, to which I attempted giving an embodied vehicle in rhyme ... Thus with me began Love and Poesy ...

> to Dr John Moore, 2 August 1787

Ay waukin, O,
    Waukin still and weary;
Sleep I can get nane
    For thinking on my dearie.
  'Ay Waukin O'

When you whisper, or look kindly to another, it gives me a draught of damnation.

> to Margaret Chalmers (A draft found in Burns's papers, *c.* January 1787)

The sweets of love are wash'd with tears.
  'The Primrose'

What is life when wanting love?
    Night without a morning;
Love's the cloudless summer sun,
    Nature gay adorning.
  'Thine am I, My Chloris Fair'

Bonnie wee thing, cannie wee thing,
    Lovely wee thing, wert thou mine,
I wad wear thee in my bosom,
    Lest my jewel I should tine.
  'The Bonnie Wee Thing'

The sordid earthworm may profess love to a woman's person, whilst in reality his affection is centred in her pocket.

to Alison Begbie, 1781

When I think I have met with you, and have lived more of real life with you in eight days than I can do with almost anybody I meet with in eight years – when I think on the improbability of meeting you in this world again, I could sit down and cry like a child!

to Margaret Chalmers, 16 September 1788

Love is the Alpha and Omega of human enjoyment. All the pleasures, all the happiness of my humble Compeers, flow immediately and directly from this delicious source. It is that spark of celestial fire which lights up the wintry hut of Poverty and makes the cheerless mansion warm, comfortable and gay.

to Alexander Cunningham, 24 January 1789

I gaed a' waefu' gate yestreen,
    A gate I fear I'll dearly rue;
I gat my death frae twa sweet een,
    Twa lovely een o' bonnie blue.
  'I Gaed a Waefu' Gate Yestreen'

She has my heart, she has my hand,
By secret troth and honour's band;
Till the mortal stroke shall lay me low,
I'm thine, my Highland lassie, O.
  'My Highland Lassie O'

My Mary! dear departed shade!
    Where is thy place of blissful rest?
See'st thou thy lover lowly laid?
    Hear'st thou the groans that rend his breast?
  'To Mary in Heaven'

Lassie wi' the lint-white locks,
    Bonie lassie, artless lassie,
Wilt thou wi' me tent the flocks,
    Wilt thou be my dearie, O?
    'Lassie wi' the Lint-white Locks'

The Kirk an' State may join an' tell,
    To do sic things I mauna;
The Kirk an' State may gae to hell,
    And I'll gae to my Anna.
    'The Gowden Locks of Anna'

Let not Woman e'er complain
    Of inconstancy in love;
Let not Woman e'er complain
    Fickle man is apt to rove;
Look abroad thro' Nature's range,
Nature's mighty law is change,
Ladies would it not seem strange
    Man should then a monster prove?
    'Let Not Woman E'er Complain'

Mankind

Good lord, what is man! for as simple he looks,
Do but try to develop his hooks and his crooks,
With his depths and his shallows, his good and his
    evil,
All in all, he's a problem must puzzle the devil.
    'Sketch, Inscribed to the Rt. Hon. Ch[arles] J. Fox Esq.'

It's coming yet, for a' that,
That man to man the world o'er
    Shall brithers be for a' that.
    'For a' That and a' That'

Man's inhumanity to man
    Makes countless thousands mourn.
  'Man was Made to Mourn'

Mankind are by nature benevolent creatures, except in a few scoundrelly instances, I do not think that avarice of the good things we chance to have is born with us; but we are placed here amid so much Nakedness, and Hunger, and Poverty, and Want, that we are under a damning necessity of studying Selfishness, in order that we may exist! Still, there are, in every age, a few souls, that all the Wants and Woes of life cannot debase to Selfishness, or even give the necessary alloy of Caution and Prudence. If ever I am in danger of vanity, it is when I contemplate myself on this side of my disposition and character. God knows I am no Saint; I have a whole host of Follies and Sins to answer for; but if I could, and I believe I do it as far as I can, I would wipe away all tears from all eyes.
    to Peter Hill, 2 March 1790

Manners
So little am I acquainted with the Modes and Manners of the mere public and polished walks of life, that I often feel myself much embarrassed how to express the feelings of my heart, particularly Gratitude.
    to James Sibbald, January 1787

I never, my friend, thought Mankind very capable of anything generous; but the stateliness of the Patricians of Edinburgh, and the servility of my plebian brethren ... have nearly put me out of conceit altogether with my species.
    to William Nicol, 18 June 1787

Marriage

Matrimony is quite a different thing from what your love-sick youths and sighing girls take it to be!

to Alexander Cunningham, 10 September 1792

I had long had a wishing eye to that inestimable blessing, a wife. My mouth watered deliciously, to see a young fellow, after a few idle commonplace stories from a gentleman in black, strip and go to bed with a young girl, and no one durst say, black was his eye; while I, for just doing the same thing, only wanting that ceremony, am made a Sunday's laughing-stock, and abused like a pickpocket.

to John Arnot, April 1786

I am but a younger son of the house of Parnassus, and, like other younger sons of great families, I may intrigue, if I choose to run all risks, but must not marry.

to James Smith, 30 June 1787

So to let you a little into the secrets of my Pericranium, there is, you know, a certain clean-limbed, handsome, bewitching young Hussy of your acquaintance, to whom I have lately, and privately given a matrimonial title to my Corpus.

to James Smith, 28 April 1788

I am so enamoured with a certain girl's prolific twin-bearing merit, that I have given her a *legal* title to the best blood in my body; and so farewell Rakery!

to James Johnson, 25 May 1788

Circumstanced as I am, I could never have got a female Partner for life who could have entered into my favourite studies, relished my Authors, etc., without entailing on me, at the same time, expensive living, fantastic caprice, apish affectation, with all the other blessed Boarding-school acquirements, which (pardonnez-moi, Madam!) are sometimes to be found among females of the upper ranks, but almost universally pervade the Misses of the Would-be gentry. In this kind of literary, sentimental correspondence, Friendship must be my social channel; at the same time I declare to God, you are almost the [only] friend of this Kind I have. So far from tiring of your correspondence, Madam, it would be one of the greatest misfortunes that could befall me, were I to lose it.

to Mrs Dunlop, 10 August 1788

You do not tell me if you are going to be married. Depend upon it, if you do not make some damned foolish choice, it will be a very great improvement on the Dish of Life. I can speak from Experience, tho' God knows, my choice was as random as Blind-Man's-Buff. I like the idea of an honest country Rake of my acquaintance, who, like myself, married lately. Speaking to me of his late step, 'Lord, man,' says he, 'a body's baith cheaper and better sair't!'

to John Buego, 9 September 1788

You must get ready for Nithsdale as fast as possible, for I have an offer of a house in the very neighbourhood with some furniture in it … We will want a Maidservant, of consequence: if you can hear of any to hire, ask after them … I am extremely happy at the idea of your coming to Nithsdale.

to Mrs Burns, 14 October 1788

Mrs Burns is getting stout again, and laid as lustily about her today at breakfast as a Reaper from the corn-ridge. That is the peculiar privilege and blessing of our hale, sprightly damsels, that are bred among the Hay and Heather. We cannot hope for that highly polished mind, that charming delicacy of soul, which is found among the Female world in the more elevated stations of life, which is certainly by far the most bewitching charm in the famous cestus of Venus. It is indeed such an estimable treasure, that, where it can be had in its native heavenly purity, unstained by some one or other of the many shades of affectation, and unalloyed by some one or other of the many species of caprice, I declare to Heaven I would think it cheaply purchased at the expense of every other earthly good! But as this angelic creature is, I am afraid, extremely rare in any station and rank of life, and totally denied to such a humble one as mine; We meaner mortals must put up with the next rank of female excellence – as fine a figure and face we can produce as any rank of life whatever; rustic, native grace; unaffected modesty, and unsullied purity; Nature's mother-wit and the rudiments of Taste; a simplicity of soul, unsuspicious of, because unacquainted with, the crooked ways of a selfish, interested, disingenuous world; and the dearest charm of all the rest, an unyielding sweetness of disposition and generous warmth of heart, grateful for love on our part and ardently glowing with a more than equal return; these, with a healthy frame, a sound, vigorous constitution, which your ranks can scarcely ever hope to enjoy, are the charms of lovely woman in my humble walk of life.

to Mrs Dunlop, 11 April 1791

He begged for Gudesake! I wad be his wife,
    Or else I wad kill him wi' sorrow;
So e'en to preserve the poor body in life,
        I think I maun wed him tomorrow, tomorrow,
        I think I maun wed him tomorrow.
'Last May a Braw Wooer Cam doun the Lang Glen'

She is a winsome wee thing,
She is a handsome wee thing,
She is a lo'esome wee thing,
　　This sweet wee wife o' mine.
　'My Wife's a Winsome Wee Thing'

I hae a wife o' my ain,
　　I'll partake wi' naebody;
I'll take cuckold frae nane,
　　I'll gie cuckold to naebody.
　'I Hae a Wife o' my Ain'

My wife's a wanton wee thing,
　　My wife's a wanton wee thing,
My wife's a wanton wee thing,
　　She winna be guided by me …

She mind't na when I forbade her,
　　She mind't na when I forbade her,
I took a rung and I claw'd her,
　　And a braw gude bairn was she.
　'My Wife's a Wanton Wee Thing'

Ah, gentle dames! it gars me greet,
To think how mony counsels sweet,
How mony lengthen'd sage advices
The husband frae the wife despises!
　'Tam O' Shanter'

Twa bonie lads were Sandy and Jockie;
Jockie was lo'ed but Sandy unlucky;
Jockie was laird baith of hills and of vallies,
But Sandy was nought but the king o' gude fellows.

Jockie lo'ed Madgie, for Madgie had money
And Sandy lo'ed Mary, for Mary was bony;
Ane wedded for love, ane wedded for treasure,
So Jockie had siller, and Sandy had pleasure.
  'Sandy and Jockie'

Sic a wife as Willie had,
I wad na gie a button for her! …

Her nose and chin they threaten ither,
I wad na gie a button for her! …

Her face wad fyle the Logan Water,
I wad na gie a button for her.
  'Willie's Wife'

How cruel are the parents
    Who riches only prize,
And to the wealthy booby
    Poor women sacrifice!
Meanwhile, the hapless daughter
    Has but a choice of strife;
To shun a tyrant Father's hate –
    Become a wretched Wife.
  'How Cruel are the Parents'

Husband, husband, cease your strife,
    Nor longer idly rave, Sir;
Tho' I am your wedded wife,
    Yet I am not your slave, Sir.
  'My Spouse Nancy'

O ay my wife she dang me,
    An' aft my wife she bang'd me,
If ye gie sic a woman her will,
    Gude faith! she'll soon o'ergang ye.
  'Ay My Wife She Dang Me'

O that I had ne'er been married,
    I wad never had nae care,
Now I've gotten wife and bairns
      An' they cry crowdie ever mair.
        Aince crowdie, twice crowdie,
          Three times crowdie in a day;
        Gin ye crowdie ony mair,
          Ye'll crowdie a' my meal away.
  'O that I had ne'er been Married'

The lover may sparkle and glow,
    Approaching his bonie bit gay thing;
But marriage will soon let him know,
    He's gotten a bushit-up naething.
  'Extemporare to Mr Gavin Hamilton'

Prudence, the bottle, and the stew
    Are fam'd for lovers' curing.
  'To Alexander Cunningham'

That hackney'd judge of human life,
    The Preacher and the King,
Observes: 'The man that gets a wife
    He gets a noble thing.'

But how capricious are mankind,
    Now loathing, now desirous!
We married men, how oft we find
    The best of things will tire us!
  'On Marriage'

Curs'd be the man, the poorest wretch in life,
The crouching vassal to the tyrant wife,
Who has no will but by her high permission;
Who has no sixpence but in her possession;

Who must to her his dear friends secrets tell;
Who dreads a curtain-lecture worse than hell.
    'The Henpeck'd Husband'

John Anderson my jo, John
        When we were first acquent;
Your locks were like the raven,
        Your bony brow was brent;
But now your brow is beld, John,
        Your locks are like the snaw;
But blessings on your frosty pow,
        John Anderson, my jo.
    'John Anderson, My Jo'

Military Life

I have today corrected the last proof sheet of my poems
... I have both a second and a third Edition going on as
the second was begun with too small a number of copies.
The whole I have printed is three thousand. Would the
profits of that afford it, with rapture I would take your
hint of a military life, as the most congenial to my
feelings and situation of any other ...
    to Mrs Dunlop, 22 March 1787

O why the deuce should I repine,
        An' be an ill foreboder;
I'm twenty-three, and five feet nine,
        I'll go and be a sodger.
    'Extemporare'

Early in life, and all my life, I reckoned on a recruiting
drum as my forlorn hope.
    to Margaret Chalmers, 22 January 1788

Ministers

Ye ministers, come mount the pupit,
An' cry till ye be hairse an' rupit;
For *Eighty-eight* he wish'd you weel,
An' gied you a' baith gear and meal;
E'en mony a plack, an' mony a peck,
Ye ken yoursels, for little feck!
   'Elegy on the Year 1788'

As cauld a wind as ever blew;
A caulder kirk, and in't but few;
As cauld's a minister's ever spak;
Ye'se a' be het or I come back.
   'Lines Written in the Kirk of Lamington'

Nay, what are priests? those seeming godly wisemen;
What are they, pray? but spiritual Excisemen.
   'Lines Written on a Window, at the King's Arms
          Tavern, Dumfries'

But I gae mad at their grimaces,
Their sighan, cantan, grace-proud faces,
Their three-mile prayers, an' hauf-mile graces,
    Their raxan conscience,
Whase greed, revenge, an' pride disgraces
    Waur nor their nonsense …

They take religion in their mouth;
They talk o' mercy, grace an' truth,
For what? – to gie their malice skouth
    On some puir wight,
An' hunt him down, o'er right an' ruth,
    To ruin streight.
   to the Reverend John M'Math enclosing a copy of *Holy*
       Willie's Prayer, which he had requested, 17
       September 1785

Now a' the congregation o'er,
    Is silent expectation;
For Moodie speels the holy door,
    Wi' tidings o' damnation;
Should *Hornie*, as in ancient days,
'Mang sons o' God present him,
The vera sight o' Moodie's face,
      To's ain *het hame* had sent him
        Wi' fright that day.

Hear how he clears the points o' Faith
    Wi' rattlin an' thumpin!
Now meekly calm, now wild in wrath,
    He's stampan, an' he's jumpan!
His lengthened chin, his turn'd up snout,
    His eldritch Squeal an' gestures,
O how they fire the heart devout,
      Like cantharidian plaisters,
        On sic a day!
  'The Holy Fair'

As for your priesthood, I shall say but little,
Corbies and *Clergy* are a shot right kittle.
  'The Twa Brigs'

Some books are lies frae end to end,
And some great lies were never penn'd;
Ev'n Ministers they hae been kenn'd,
    In holy rapture,
A rousing whid, at times to vend,
    And nail't wi' Scripture.
  'Death and Dr Hornbrook'

Here sowter xxxx in Death does sleep;
    To Hell, if he's gane thither,

Satan, gie him thy gear to keep,
    He'll haud it weel thegither.
   'On a Celebrated Ruling Elder'

The minister kiss'd the fiddler's wife,
An' couldna preach for thinkin' o't.
   'My Love she's but a Lassie Yet'

Poet Burns! poet Burns, wi' your priest-skelping
     turns,
    Why desert ye your auld native shire?
Your muse is a gypsy, yet were she e'en tipsy,
    She could ca' us nae waur than we are, Poet
    Burns,
She could ca' us nae waur than we are.
   'The Kirk's Alarm'

Money

I never was cannie for hoarding o' money,
    Or claughtin't together at a', man,
I've little to spend and naething to lend,
    But devil a shilling I awe, man.
   'The Ronalds of the Benals'

I now see it improbable that I shall ever acquire riches, and am therefore endeavouring to gather a philosophical contempt of enjoyment so hard to be gained and so easily lost.
   to William Niven, 3 November 1780

To be rich and to be great are the grand concerns of this world's men, and to be sure if moderately pursued it is laudable; but where is it moderately pursued? The greater part of men grasp at riches as eagerly as if Poverty were but another word for Damnation and misery; whereas I affirm that the man whose only wish is to become great and rich ... whatever he may pretend to be, at the bottom he is but a miserable wretch. Avoid this sordid turn of mind if you would be happy.

to Thomas Orr, 7 September 1782

I assure you, my dear Sir, that you truly hurt me with your pecuniary parcel. It degrades me in my own eyes. However, to return it would savour of bombast affectation. But, as to any more traffic of that Dr and Cr kind, I swear, by that Honour which crowns the upright Statue of Robert Burns's Integrity! – On the least motion of it, I will indignantly spurn the by-past transaction, and from that moment commence entire Stranger to you.

to George Thomson, July 1793

This is a painful, disagreeable letter; and first of the kind I ever wrote. I am truly in serious distress for three or four guineas; can you, my dear Sir, accommodate me?

to William Stewart, 15 January 1795

It is needless to attempt an apology for my remissness to you in money-matters. Sir, I had it not. The distressful state of Commerce at this town has this year literally taken from my otherwise scanty income no less than 20£. That part of my Salary depended upon Imports, and they are no more, for one year. I enclose you three guineas, and shall settle all with you.

to Captain John Hamilton, 29 January 1795

When you offered me money-assistance little did I think I should want it so soon. A rascal of a Haberdasher to whom I owe a considerable bill taking it into his head that I am dying, has commenced a process against me and will, infallibly put my emaciated body into jail. Will you be so good as to accommodate me, and that by return of post, with ten pound?

to James Burness, 12 July 1796

After all my boasted independence, curst necessity compels me to implore you for five pounds ... Do, for God's sake, send me that sum, and that by return of post. Forgive me this earnestness, but the horrors of a jail have made me half distracted.

to George Thomson, 12 July 1796

Morality

Ye'll get the best o' moral works,
'Mang black Gentoos, and pagan Turks,
Or hunters wild on Ponotoxy,
Wha never heard of orthodoxy ...

Morality, thou deadly bane
Thy tens o' thousands thou hast slain!
Vain is his hope, whose stay an' trust is,
In moral mercy, truth and justice!
'A Dedication to Gavin Hamilton'

Music

I am in hopes that I shall pick up some fine tunes from among the Collection of Highland Airs which I got from you at Edinburgh. I have had an able Fiddler two days already on it, and I expect him every day for another review of it.

to James Johnson, July 1788

Be not in a hurry; let us go on correctly; and your name shall be immortal! ... I see every day, new Musical Publications, advertised; but what are they? Gaudy, hunted butterflies of a day, and then vanish for ever; but your work [*The Scots Musical Museum*] will outlive the momentary neglects of idle Fashion, and defy the teeth of time.

to James Johnson, 18 November 1788

But let me remark to you, in the sentiment and style of our Scottish airs, there is a pastoral simplicity, a something that one may call, the Doric style and dialect of vocal music, to which a dash of our native tongue and manners is particularly, nay, peculiarly apposite.

to George Thomson, 26 October 1792

The compass of the heart, in the musical style of expression, is much more bounded, than the reach of invention; so the notes of the former are extremely apt to run into similar passages; but in return for the paucity of its compass, its few notes are much more sweet.

to Mrs Dunlop, 6 December 1792

I have still several MSS Scots airs by me, which I have picked up, mostly from the singing of country lasses. They please me vastly; but your learned lugs would perhaps be displeased with the very feature for which I like them. I call them simple; you would pronounce them silly.

to George Thomson, April 1793

Whatever Mr Pleyel does, let him not alter one iota of the original Scots Air ... Let our National Music preserve its native features. They are, I own, frequently wild, and unreduceable to the modern rules; but on that very eccentricity, perhaps, depends a great part of their effect.

to George Thomson, 26 April 1793

You know that my pretensions to musical taste, are merely a few of Nature's instincts, untaught and untutored by Art. For this reason, many musical compositions, particularly where much of the merit lies in Counterpoint, however they may transport and ravish the ears of you, Connoisseurs, affect my simple lug no otherwise than merely as Din.

to George Thomson, *c.* 30 August 1793

I was much obliged to you, dear friend, for making me acquainted with Gow. He is a modest, intelligent, worthy fellow; besides his being a man of great genius in his way. I have spent many happy hours with him, in the short while he has been here.

to James Johnson, October 1793

I am sensible that my taste in Music must be inelegant and vulgar, because people of undisputed and cultivated taste can find no merit in many of my favourite tunes. Still, because I am cheaply pleased, is that any reason why I should deny myself that pleasure? Many of our Strathspeys, ancient and modern, give me most exquisite enjoyment, where you and other judges would probably be showing signs of disgust.

to George Thomson, September 1794

Nature

In vain do we talk of reason … We are the offspring of caprice, and the nurslings of habitude. The most pleasurable part of our existence, the strings that tie heart to heart, are the manufacture of some hitherto undescribed and unknown power within us. The circle of our acquaintance, like a wide horizon, is too large for us to make anything of it. We are amused for a little with the ill-defined, distant objects; but our tired eye soon

fixes with delighted discrimination on the towering cliffs, or the winding river, a hoary ruin, or a woody vale, just as that nameless something within us directs.
    to William Dunbar, early February 1789

Where braving angry winter's storms,
    The lofty Ochils rise …
    'Braving Angry Winter's Storms'

Loud blaws the frosty breezes,
    The snaws the mountain cover.
    'The Young Highland Rover'

The Catrine woods were yellow seen,
    The flowers decay'd on Catrine lee,
Nae laverock sang on hillock green,
    But nature sicken'd on the e'e.
    'Farewell to Ballochmyle'

Fair is a morn in flow'ry May,
    And sweet an ev'n in autumn mild;
When roving thro' the garden gay
    Or wand'ring in the lonely wild.
    'The Lass o Ballochmyle'

O Nature! a' thy shews an' forms
To feeling pensive hearts hae charms!
Whether the summer kindly warms,
    Wi' life an' light;
Or winter's howls, in gusty storms,
    The lang, dark night!
    'Epistle to William Simson'

Yesternight until a very late hour did I wait with anxious horror, for the appearance of some Comet firing half the sky; or aerial armies of sanguinary Scandinavians, darting athwart the startled heavens rapid as the ragged lightning, and horrid as those convulsions of Nature that bury nations. The elements, however, seem to take the matter very quietly: they did not even usher in this morning with triple suns and a shower of blood, symbolical of the three potent heroes and the mighty claret-shed of the day.

to Captain Robert Riddell, 16 October 1789

Parenthood

On the 13 Currt I lost the best of fathers. Though to be sure we have had long warning of the impending stroke still, the tender feelings of Nature claim their part and I cannot recollect the tender endearments and parental lessons of the best of friends and the ablest of instructors without feeling, what perhaps the calmer dictates of reason would partly condemn.

to James Burness, 17 February 1784

Life, my dear Sir, is a serious matter. You know by experience that a man's individual self is a good deal, but, believe me, a wife and family of children, whenever you have the honour to be a husband and a father, will shew you that your present and most anxious hours of solicitude are spent on trifles. The welfare of those who are very dear to us, whose only support, hope and stay we are – this, to a generous mind, is another sort of more important object of care than any concerns whatever which centre merely in the individual.

to Robert Ainslie, 8 June 1789

The grateful reverence to the hoary, earthly Authors of his being – The burning glow when he clasps the Woman of his Soul to his bosom – the tender yearnings of heart for the little Angels to whom he has given existence

These, Nature has pour'd in milky streams about the human heart; and the Man who never rouses them into action by the inspiring influences of their proper objects, loses by far the most pleasurable part of his existence.
to John Kennedy, 26 September 1786

By the way, I hear I am a girl out of pocket and by careless, murdering mischance too, which has provoked me and vexed me a good deal.
to John Richmond, 25 October 1787

What a life of solicitude is the life of a parent!
to Mrs Dunlop, 27 September 1788

You have a little miscalculated my feelings, my honoured friend, respecting the naming of my child. To name my child after any of the Great, with a view to their future benificence, is quite foreign to my ideas; my motive is gratitude, not selfishness. Though I may die a Poor Man, yet I hope my children shall ever boast the character of their Father; and as that father has some few in the upper ranks of life to whom he is peculiarly indebted, or whom he holds peculiarly dear, he wishes his children to indulge an honest pride on that account; and not only as a memento of these honours their father enjoyed, but as an incentive to noble action, he will call his children after the names of his illustrious friends and benefactors.
to Mrs Dunlop, 25 March 1789

I wish I had lived in the days of Joktan, in whose days, says Moses, the earth was divided. Then a patriarchal fellow like me might have been the father of a nation.
to Mrs Dunlop, 21 April 1789

I am resolved never to breed up a Son of mine to any of the learned Professions. I know the value of independence; and since I cannot give my Sons an independent fortune, I shall give them an independent line of life. What a chaos of hurry, chance and change is this world, when one sits soberly down to reflect on it! To a Father who himself knows the world, the thought that he shall have Sons to usher into it, must fill him with dread; but if he have Daughters, the prospect in a thoughtful moment is apt to shock him.

to William Dunbar, 2 February 1790

There had much need be many pleasures annexed to the state of husband and father, for God knows, they have many peculiar cares. I cannot describe to you, the anxious, sleepless hours these ties frequently give me. I see a train of helpless little folks; me, and my exertions, all their stay; and on what a brittle thread does the life of man hang! If I am nipped off at the command of Fate; even in all the vigour of manhood as I am, such things happen every day – gracious God! what would become of my little flock! 'Tis here I envy your people of fortune. A Father on his deathbed, taking an everlasting leave of his children, is indeed woe enough; but the man of competent fortune leaves his sons and daughters independency and friends, while I – but, my God, I shall run distracted if I think any longer on the subject!

to Mrs Dunlop, 15 December 1793

Philosophy

Whistle o'er the lave o't!
  'Whistle O'er the Lave O't'

I'll no say, men are villains a';
  The real, harden'd wicked,

Wha hae nae check but human law,
    Are to a few restricked;
But, och! mankind are unco weak,
    An' little to be trusted;
If *self* the wavering balance shake,
    It's rarely right adjusted! ...

Ay free, aff han', your story tell,
    When wi' a bosom crony;
But still keep something to yoursel
    Ye scarcely tell to ony;
Conceal yoursel as weel's ye can
    Frae critical dissection;
But keek thro' ev'ry other man
    Wi' sharpen'd sly inspection.
    'Epistle to a Young Friend'

Facts are chiels that winna ding;
    An' downa be disputed.
    'A Dream'

Then at the balance let's be mute,
    We never can adjust it;
What's done we partly may compute,
    But know not what's resisted.
    'Address to the Unco Guid'

Aft a ragged cowt's been known
    To mak a noble aiver.
    'A Dream'

Know prudent, cautious self-control
    Is wisdom's root.
    'A Bard's Epitaph'

A few honest Prejudices and benevolent Prepossessions, are of the utmost consequence, and give the finishing polish to the illustrious characters of Patriot, Benefactor, Father and Friend ...
>to Mrs Dunlop, 21 June 1789

No man knows what Nature has fitted him for until he try.
>to Lady Elizabeth Cunningham, 23 December 1789

Virtue and study are their own reward.
>to Lady Elizabeth Cunningham, 23 December 1789

> Then let us pray that come it may
>   (As come it will for a' that),
> That Sense and Worth, o'er a' the earth
>   Shall bear the gree, an' a' that.
> For a' that, an' a' that,
>   It's comin' yet for a' that,
> That Man to Man, the warld o'er
>   Shall brithers be for a' that.
>   'A Man's a Man for a' That'

> The best laid schemes o' mice and men
>   Gang aft a-gley.
>   'To a Mouse'

> But *human bodies* are sic fools,
> For a' their Colleges an' Schools,
> That when nae *real* ills perplex them,
> They mak enow themselves to vex them;
> An' ay the less they hae to sturt them,
> In like proportion, less will hurt them.
>   'The Twa Dogs'

For thus the royal *Mandate* ran,
When first the human race began,
'The social, friendly, honest man,
    Whate'er he be,
'Tis *he* fulfils *great Nature's plan*,
    And none but *he*.'
    'Second Epistle to John Lapraik'

We ought, when we wish to be economists in happiness;
we ought in the first place to fix the standard of our own
character; and when ... we know where we stand, and
how much ground we occupy, let us contend for it as
property; and those who seem to doubt, or deny us what
is justly ours, let us either pity their prejudices or despise
their judgement.
    to Mrs M'Lehose, 7 March 1788

The language of refusal is to me the most difficult
language on earth.
    to Gavin Hamilton, 7 March 1788

And may ye better reck the rede
Than ever did the adviser.
    'Epistle to a Young Friend 1786'

O ye douce folk that live by rule,
Grave, tideless-blooded, calm an' cool,
Compar'd wi' you – O fool! fool! fool!
    How much unlike!
Your hearts are just a standing pool,
    Your lives, a dyke!
    'Epistle to James Smith'

A few days may – a few years must –
Repose us in the silent dust.
   'Sketch   New Years Day   to Mrs Dunlop'

O wad some Pow'r the giftie gie us
To see oursels as others see us!
It wad frae mony a blunder free us
    An' foolish notion.
   'To a Louse'

Nae man can tether time or tide.
   'Tam O' Shanter'

Time but the impression deeper makes,
As streams their channels deeper wear.
   'To Mary in Heaven'

I have often in Poetic frenzy looked on this world as one
vast ocean, occupied and commoved by innumerable
vortices, each whirling round its centre, which vortices
are the children of men; and that the great design, and
merit if I may say so, of every particular vortex consists,
in how wide it can extend the influence of its circle, and
how much floating trash it can suck in and absorb.
   to Robert Graham, 31 July 1789

To give my counsels all in one,
Thy tuneful flame still careful fan;
Preserve the dignity of Man,
    With soul erect;
And trust the Universal Plan
    Will all protect.
   'The Vision'

Then gently scan your brother Man,
    Still gentler sister Woman;
Tho' they may gang a kennin wrang
    To step aside is human:
One point must still be greatly dark,
    The moving *Why* they do it;
And just as lamely can ye mark
    How far perhaps they rue it.

Who made the heart, 'tis he alone
    Decidedly can try us;
He knows each cord, its various tone,
    Each spring its various bias;
Then at the balance let's be mute,
    We never can adjust it;
What's done we partly may compute,
    But know not what's resisted.
  'Address to the Unco Guid'

What mischiefs daily arise from silly garrulity, or foolish confidence! There is an excellent Scots Saying, that 'A man's mind is his kingdom.' It is certainly so; but how far can he govern that kingdom with propriety.
    to William Burns, 10 March 1789

And let us mind, faint heart ne'er wan
    A lady fair;
Wha does the utmost that he can,
    Will whyles do mair.
    to Dr Blacklock

God knows I am no Saint; I have a whole host of Follies and Sins to answer for.
    to Peter Hill, 2 March 1790

There are not any first principles or component parts of the Human Mind, more truly radical than what is meant by OUGHT, and, OUGHT NOT; which mankind … have, for several thousand years, agreed are synonymous terms with Virtue, and Vice. But, except for our Existence *here*, have a reference to existence *hereafter*, whole of the drama, then a man's individual Self, his own pleasures and enjoyments, are and should be the whole of his care; and the true standard of his actions is, Proper and Improper.

to Mrs Dunlop, 9 July 1790

We wrap ourselves up in a cloak of our own better fortune, and turn away our eyes, lest the wants and woes of our brother-mortals should disturb the selfish apathy of our souls.

to Crauford Tait, 15 October 1790

In such a bad world as ours, those who add to the scanty sum of our pleasures, are positively our benefactors.

to Miss Louisa Fontenelle, *c.* November 1792

Of all the qualities we assign to the Author and Director of Nature, by far the most enviable is, to be able to 'wipe away all tears from all eyes'. O what insignificant, sordid wretches are they, however chance may have loaded them with wealth, who go to their graves, to their magnificent mausoleums, with hardly the consciousness of having made one poor honest heart happy!

to Mrs Maria Riddell, November 1792

Places

This country has nothing new. Mankind are the same everywhere. In this place [Dumfries], as in Glasgow I suppose too, of the men called honest, and the women called chaste, a number supposed to be near the full half of them are not what they pretend to be; and of the remaining half, many of them are thought to have still worse faults.

to James Hamilton, 27 April 1789

My loins are girded, my sandals on my feet and my staff in my hand; and in half an hour I shall set off from this venerable, respectable, hospitable, social, convivial, imperial Queen of cities, Auld Reekie ...

Now, God in heaven bless Reekie's town
    With plenty, joy and peace!
And may her wealth and fair renown
    To latest times increase!!! – Amen.

to M. Fyffe, 5 May 1787

Thy sons, Edina, social, kind,
    With open arms the stranger hail ...

Edina! *Scotia's* darling seat!
    All hail thy palaces and tow'rs,
Where once, beneath a Monarch's feet
    Sat legislation's sov'reign powers!

'Address to Edinburgh'

London swarms with worthless wretches who prey on their fellow-creatures' thoughtlessness or inexperience.

to William Burns, 10 February 1790

Ramsay an' famous Fergusson
Gied Forth and Tay a lift aboon;
Yarrow an' Tweed, to monie a tune,
    Owre Scotland rings;
While Irwin, Lugar, Ayr an' Doon
    Naebody sings ...

We'll sing auld Coila's plains an' fells,
Her moors red-brown wi' heather bells,
Her banks an' braes, her dens an' dells,
     Where glorious Wallace
Aft bure the gree, as story tells,
     Frae Suthron billies.
  'To William Simson'

There is a small river, Afton, that falls into Nith, near
New Cumnock; which has some charming, wild,
romantic scenery on its banks. I have a particular
pleasure in those little pieces of poetry such as our Scots
songs etc., where the names and landskip – features of
rivers, lakes, or woodlands that one knows, are
introduced. I attempted a compliment of that kind to
Afton as follows: I mean it for Johnson's Musical
Museum.

  Flow gently, clear Afton, among thy green braes.
    to Mrs Dunlop, 5 February 1789

It's up wi' the Sutors o' Selkirk,
     And down wi' the Earl o' Hume;
And here is to a' the braw laddies
     That wear the single sol'd shoon:
It's up wi' the Sutors o' Selkirk,
     For they are baith trusty and leal;
And up wi' the lads o' the Forest,
     And down wi' the Merse to the deil.
  'Sutors o' Selkirk'

Now Simmer blinks on flowery braes,
And o'er the crystal streamlet plays;
Come, let us spend the lightsome days,
     In the birks of Aberfeldy.
  'The Birks o' Aberfeldy'

I write this on a tour where savage streams tumble over savage mountains, thinly overspread with savage flocks, which starvingly support as savage inhabitants. My last stage was Inverary – tomorrow night's stage, Dumbarton.

to Robert Ainslie, Arrochar, 25 June 1787

Who'er he be that sojourns here,
    I pity much his case,
Unless he come to wait upon
    The lord *their* god, 'His Grace.'

There's naething here but Highland pride,
    And Highland scab and hunger!
If Providence has sent me here,
    'Twas surely in an anger.
  'The Bard at Inverary'

We cam na here to view your warks,
    In hopes to be mair wise,
But only, lest we gang to hell,
    It may be nae surprise:
But when we tirl'd at your door
    Your porter dought na hear us;
Sae may, shou'd we to hell's yetts come,
    Your billy Satan sair us!
  'Impromptu on Carron Iron Works'

Auld Ayr, wham ne'er a town surpasses,
For honest men and bonny lasses.
  'Tam O' Shanter'

The banks of the Nith are as sweet, poetic ground as any I ever saw.

to Patrick Miller, 20 October 1787

I am quite charmed with the Dumfries folk.
>to William Nicol, 18 June 1787

Pleasure

Chords that vibrate sweetest pleasure,
    Thrill the deepest notes of woe.
>'Poem on Sensibility'

But pleasures are like poppies spread –
You seize the flower, its bloom is shed;
Or like the snow falls in the river –
A moment white – then melts for ever.
>'Tam O' Shanter'

I saw thy pulse's maddening play,
Wild-send thee Pleasure's devious way,
Misled by fancy's meteor ray,
    By passion driven;
But yet the light that led astray
    Was light from heaven.
>'The Vision: Duan 2'

Poetry

The Muse, nae poet ever fand her,
Till by himself he learned to wander,
Adown some trottin burn's meander,
    An' no think lang.
>to William Simson

Do you recollect a Sunday we spent in Eglinton woods?
You told me, on my repeating some verses to you, that
you wondered I could resist the temptation of sending
verse of such merit to a magazine; 'twas actually this that
gave me an idea of my own pieces, which encouraged me
to endeavour at the character of a poet.
>to Captain Richard Brown, 30 December 1787

Leeze me on rhyme! it's aye a treasure,
My chief, amaist my only pleasure;
At hame, a-fiel, at wark, or leisure,
    The Muse, poor hizzie!
Tho' rough an' raploch be her measure,
    She's seldom lazy.
  'Second Epistle to Davie'

I've seen me daez't upon a time,
I scarce could wink or see a styme;
Just ae half-mutchkin does me prime,
    (Ought less, is little),
Then back I rattle on the rhyme,
    As gleg's a whistle.
  'Epistle to John Goldie'

Some rhyme a neebour's name to lash
Some rhyme (vain thought!) for needfu' cash;
Some rhyme to court the countra clash,
    An' raise a din;
For me, an aim I never fash;
    I rhyme for fun.
  'Epistle to James Smith'

Tho' I should wander *Terra* o'er,
    In all her climes,
Grant me but this, I ask no more,
    Ay rowth o' rhymes.
  'Epistle to James Smith'

The poet may jingle and rhyme,
    In hopes of a laureate wreathing,
And when he has wasted his time,
    He's kindly rewarded wi' – naething.
  'Stanzas on Naething'

Curse on ungrateful man, that can be pleased,
And yet can starve the author of the pleasure!
O thou, my elder brother in misfortune,
By far my elder brother in the Muse,
With tears I pity thy unhappy fate!
Why is the Bard unfited by the world,
Yet has so keen a relish of its pleasures?
   Inscribed under Fergusson's Portrait

Thou, Nature, partial nature, I arraign,
Of thy caprice maternal I complain.
The lion and the bull thy care have found,
One shakes the forest, and one spurns the ground:
Thou giv'st the ass his hide, the snail his shell,
Th' envenom'd wasp, victorious, guards his cell,
Thy minions, kings defend, control, devour,
In all the omnipotence of rule and power.
Foxes and statesmen, subtle wiles ensure;
The cit and polecat stink, and are secure.
Toads with their poison, doctors with their drug,
The priest and hedgehog in their robes are snug.
Even silly woman has her warlike arts
Her tongue and eyes, her dreaded spear and darts.

But O! thou bitter step-mother and hard,
To thy poor, fenceless, naked child – the Bard!
A thing unteachable, in world's skill,
An half an idiot too, more helpless still.
   'To Robert Graham of Fintry Esquire 1791'

With arch-alacrity, and conscious glee,
(Nature may have her whim as well as we);
Her Hogarth-art perhaps she meant to show;
She forms the thing, and christens it – a Poet;
Creature, tho' oft the prey of care and sorrow,
When blest today, unmindful of tomorrow;

A being formed t'amuse his grave friends,
Admired and praised – and there the wages end;
A mortal quite unfit for fortune's strife,
Yet oft the sport of all the ills of life;
Prone to enjoy each pleasure riches give,
Yet haply wanting wherewithal to live;
Longing to wipe each tear, to heal each groan,
Yet frequent all-unheeded in his own.
　　'To Robert Graham of Fintry Esquire 1788'

Shenstone observes finely that love-verses writ without any real passion are the most nauseous of all conceits; and I have often thought that no man can be a proper critic of Love compositions, except he himself, in one, or more instances, have been a warm votary of this passion. As I have been all along, a miserable dupe to Love, and have been led into a thousand weaknesses and follies by it, for that reason I put the more confidence in my critical skill in distinguishing foppery and conceit, from real passion and nature.
　　First Commonplace Book, April 1784

Poets ... of all Mankind, feel most forcibly the powers of BEAUTY; as, if they are really Poets of Nature's making, their feelings must be finer, and their taste more delicate than most of the world.
　　to Margaret Kennedy, Autumn 1785

There is a pretty large portion of bedlam in the composition of a Poet at any time ...
　　to John Arnot, *c*. April 1786

Poets are such outré beings, so much the children of wayward fancy and capricious whim, that I believe the world generally allows them a larger latitude in the rules of propriety, than the sober sons of Judgement and Prudence.

to Wilhelmina Alexander, 8 November 1786

I do not think prodigality is, by any means, a necessary concomitant of a poetic turn, but I believe a careless, indolent attention to economy is almost inseparable from it; then there must be in the heart of every bard of Nature's making, a certain modest sensibility, mixed with a kind of pride, that will ever keep him out of the way of those windfalls of fortune which frequently light on hardy impudence and foot-licking servility.

to Sir John Whiteford, 1 December 1786

I have long studied myself, and I think I know pretty exactly what ground I occupy, both as a Man and a Poet; and however the world, or a friend, may sometimes differ from me in that particular, I stand for it, in silent resolve, with all the tenaciousness of Property.

to William Greenfield, December 1786

The novelty of a Poet in my obscure situation, without any of these advantages which are reckoned necessary for that character, at least at this time of day, has raised a partial tide of public notice which has borne me to a height, where I am absolutely, feelingly certain my abilities are inadequate to support me; and too surely do I see that time when the tide will leave me, and recede, perhaps, as far below the mark of truth.

to Mrs Dunlop, 15 January 1787

The hope to be admired for ages is, in by far the greater part of what are to even authors of repute, an unsubstantial dream.

to Dr John Moore, January 1787

I am very willing to admit that I have some poetical abilities; and as few, if any Writers ... are intimately acquainted with the classes of Mankind among whom I have chiefly mingled, I may have seen men and manners in a different phasis, which may assist originality of thought.

to Dr John Moore, January 1787

I scorn the affectation of seeming modesty to cover self-conceit. That I have some merit I do not deny; but I see with frequent wringings of heart, that the novelty of my character, and the honest national prejudice of my countrymen, have borne me to a height altogether untenable to my abilities.

to Dr John Moore, 15 February 1787

The appelation of a Scotch Bard is by far my highest pride; to continue to deserve it my most exalted ambition. Scottish scenes, and Scottish story are the themes I could wish to sing.

to Mrs Dunlop, 22 March 1787

I do not intend to give up Poesy; being bred to labour secures me independence, and the muses are my chief, sometimes have been my only enjoyment.

to Mrs Dunlop, 22 March 1787

Those who think that composing a Scotch song is a trifling business, let them try.

to James Hoy, 6 November 1787

To know myself had been all along my constant study. I weighed myself alone; I balanced myself with others; I watched every means of information how much ground I occupied as a Man and as a Poet ... I was pretty sure my Poems would meet with some applause ... I threw off six hundred copies, of which I had got subscriptions for about three hundred and fifty. My vanity was highly gratified by the reception I met with from the Public; besides pocketing, all expenses deducted, near twenty pounds.

> to Dr John Moore, 2 August 1787
> (of the Kilmarnock Poems)

Poesy was still a darling walk for my mind, but 'twas only the humour of the hour. I had usually half a dozen or more pieces on hand; I took up one or other as it suited the momentary tone of the mind, and dismissed it as it bordered on fatigue.

> to Dr John Moore, 2 August 1787
> (of himself at 22)

Rhyme is the coin with which a Poet pays his debts of honour or gratitude.

> to Josiah Walker, 5 September 1787

Fiction ... is the native region of poetry.

> to Mrs Agnes M'Lehose, 6 December 1787

Finding fault with the vaguings of a poet's fancy is much such another business as Xerxes chastising the waves of Hellespont.

> to Mrs M'Lehose, 20 December 1787

> Browster wives an' whisky stills,
>> They are the muses.
> 'Third Epistle to John Lapraik'

I think it is one of the greatest pleasures attending a Poetic genius, that we can give our woes, cares, joys, loves etc., an embodied form in verse, which, to me, is ever immediate ease.

> to Mrs Agnes M'Lehose, 14 January 1788

A lame Poet is unlucky; lame verse is an everyday circumstance.

to John Richmond, 7 February 1788

The character and employment of a Poet were formerly my pleasure, but are now my pride. I know that a very great deal of my late éclat was owing to the singularity of my situation and the honest prejudice of Scotsmen; but still, as I said in the preface to my first edition, I do look upon myself as having some pretensions from Nature to the poetic character.

to Dr John Moore, 4 January 1789

Mankind in general agree in testifying their devotion, their gratitude, their friendship, or their love, by presenting whatever they hold dearest. Everybody who is the least acquainted with the character of a Poet, knows that there is nothing in the world on which he sets so much value as his verses.

to Henry Erskine, 22 January 1789

A Poet and a Beggar are in so many points of view alike, that one might take them for the same individual character under different designations; were it not that though, with a trifling Poetic licence, most Poets may be styled Beggars, yet the converse of the proposition does not hold, that every Beggar is a Poet.

to John M'Murdo, 9 January 1789

You cannot easily imagine what thin-skinned animals, what sensitive plants, poor Poets are. How we do shrink into the embittered corner of self-abasement when neglected or condemned by those to whom we look up! and how do we, in erect importance, add another cubit to our stature, on being noticed and applauded by those whom we honour and respect.

to Mrs M'Murdo, 2 May 1789

There is not among all the Martyrologies that ever were penned, so rueful a narrative as Johnson's *Lives of the Poets*. In the comparative view of Wretches, the criterion is not, what are they doomed to suffer, but how are they formed to bear. Take a being of our kind; give him a stronger imagination and more delicate sensibility, which will ever between them engender a more ungovernable set of Passions, than the usual lot of man ... send him adrift after some wayward pursuit which shall certainly mislead him from the paths of Lucre, yet, curse him with a meaner relish than any man living for the pleasures that only Lucre can bestow; lastly, fill up the measures of his woes, by bestowing on him a spurning sense of his own dignity; and you have created a wight nearly as miserable as a Poet.

    to Miss Helen Craik, 9 August 1790

For my own part, a thing that I have just composed, always appears through a double portion of that particular medium in which an Author will ever view his own Works. I believe in general, Novelty has something that inebriates the fancy; and not unfrequently dissipates and fumes away like other intoxication, and leaves the poor Patient, as usual, with an aching heart.

    to Alexander Cunningham, 11 March 1791

I have two or three times in my life composed from the wish rather than from the impulse, but I never succeeded to any purpose.

    to Alexander Cunningham, 11 March 1791

Many verses on which an author would by no means rest his reputation, in print, may yet amuse an idle moment, in manuscript ...

    to Mrs Catherine Gordon Stewart, October 1791

I have long ago made up my mind as to my own reputation in the business of Authorship; and have nothing to be pleased, or offended at, in your adoption or rejection of my verses.

    tᴄ George Thomson, 26 October 1792

You must know, that all my earlier love-songs were the breathings of ardent passion; and tho' it might have been easy in aftertimes to have given them a polish, yet that polish, to me, whose they were, and who perhaps alone cared for them, would have defaced the legend of my heart, which was so faithfully inscribed on them.

    to George Thomson, 27 October 1792

You cannot imagine how much this business of composing for your publication has added to my enjoyments. What with my earlier attachment to ballads, Johnson's Museum, your book etc., Ballad-making is now as completely my hobby-horse, as ever Fortification was Uncle Toby's; so I'll e'en canter it away till I come to the last limit of my race, (God grant that I may take the right side of the winning-post!) and then cheerfully looking back on the honest folks with whom I have been happy, I shall say, or sing, 'Sae merry as we a' hae been', and then, raising my last looks to the whole Human race, the last voice of Coila shall be – 'Goodnight and joy be wi' you a' '. So much for my last words …

    to George Thomson, 7 April 1793

A Ballad is my hobby-horse, which, though otherwise a simple sort of harmless, idiotical beast enough, has yet this blessed headstrong property, that when once it has fairly made off with a hapless wight, it gets so enamoured with the tinkle-gingle, tinkle-gingle of its own bells, that it is sure to run poor Pilgarlick, the bedlam Jockey, quite beyond any useful point or part in the common race of Man.

> to George Thomson, September 1793

Autumn is my propitious season. I make more verses in it, than all the year else.

> to George Thomson, 19 August 1793

By the bye, I am a good deal luckier than most poets. When I sing of Miss Davies or Miss Lesley Baillie, I have only to feign the passion – the charms are real.

> to Miss Deborah Duff Davies, June 1793

I muse and rhyme, morning, noon and night; and have a hundred different poetic plans, pastoral, georgic, dramatic, and etc., floating in the regions of fancy, somewhere between Purpose and resolve.

> to Lady Elizabeth Cunningham, 22 January 1789

Politics

It's hardly in a body's pow'r,
To keep, at times, frae being sour,
    To see how things are shar'd;
How best o' chiels are whyles in want,
While coofs on countless thousands rant,
    And ken na how to ware't:
But, Davie, lad, ne'er fash your head,
  Tho' we hae little gear;
We're fit to win our daily bread,
    As lang's we're hale and fier …

It's no in titles, nor in rank;

It's no in wealth like Lon'on bank,
    To purchase peace and rest;
It's no in makin' muckle mair;
It's no in books, it's no in lear,
    To make us truly blest:
If happiness hae not her seat
    An' centre in the breast,
We may be wise, or rich, or great,
    But never can be blest;
        Nae treasures, nor pleasures,
            Could make us happy lang;
        The heart ay's the part ay
            That makes us right or wrang.
  'Epistle to Davie, a Brother Poet'

Pray Billy Pit explain thy rigs,
    This new poll-tax of thine!
'I mean to mark the GUINEA PIGS
    From other common SWINE!'
    'On Mr Pitt's Hair-Powder Tax'

This mony a day I've grain'd and gaunted,
To ken what French mischief was brewin;
Or what the drumlie Dutch were doin;
That vile doup-skelper, Emperor Joseph,
If Venus yet had got his nose off;
Or how the collieshangie works
Atween the Russians and the Turks;
Or if the Swede, before he halt,
Would play another Charles the twalt;
If Denmark, any body spak o't;
Or Poland, wha had now the tack o't;
How cut-throat Prussian blades were hingin;
How libbet Italy was singin;
If Spaniard, Portuguese, or Swiss,

141

Were sayin or takin aught amiss;
Or how our merry lads at hame,
In Britain's court kept up the game.
> to a Gentleman who had sent him a newspaper, and
> offered to continue it free of charge

But Politics, truce! we're on dangerous ground;
    Who knows how the fashions may alter;
The doctrines today that are loyally sound,
    Tomorrow may bring us a halter.
> Epistle to Mr Tytler of Woodhouselee, author of a
> *Defence of Mary, Queen of Scots*

In politics if thou would'st mix,
    And mean thy fortunes be;
Bear this in mind, be deaf and blind,
    Let great folks hear and see.
> Untitled

Politics is dangerous ground for me to tread on, and yet
I cannot for the soul of me resist an impulse of anything
like wit.
> to Mrs Dunlop, 3 April 1789

I am too little a man to have any political attachments; I
am deeply indebted to, and have the warmest veneration
for, Individuals of both Parties; but a man who has it in
his power to be the Father of a Country, and who is only
known to that country by the mischiefs he does in it, is a
character of which one cannot speak with patience.
> to Robert Graham, 9 December 1789

Alas! have I often said to myself, what are all the boasted
advantages which my country reaps from the Union,
that can counterbalance the annihilation of her

Independence, and even her very name! ... Nothing can reconcile me to the common terms, 'English ambassador, English court', etc.... Tell me, friend, is this weak prejudice? I believe in my conscience such ideas as 'my country; her independence; her honour; the illustrious names that mark the history of my native land;' etc. – I believe these, among your <u>men of the world</u>, men who in fact guide for the most part and govern our world, are looked on as so many modifications of, wrongheadedness. They know the use of bawling out such terms, to rouse or lead THE RABBLE; but for their own private use, with almost all the <u>able statesmen</u> that ever existed, or now exist; when they talk of right and wrong, they only mean proper and improper; and their measure of conduct is, not what they <u>ought</u>, but what they <u>dare.</u>

    to Mrs Dunlop, 10 April 1790

Out upon the world! says I: that its affairs are administered so ill! They talk of REFORM – My God! What a reform I would make among the Sons, and even the Daughters, of men! Down, immediately, should go Fools from the high places where misbegotten Chance has perked them up; and through life should they skulk, ever haunted by their native insignificance, as the body marches accompanied by its shadow.

    to Miss Deborah Duff Davies, 6 April 1793

> We labour soon, we labour late,
>   To feed the titled knave, man;
> And a' the comfort we're to get,
>   Is that ayont the grave, man.
>   'The Tree of Liberty'

In the year 1792–3, when Royalist and Jacobin had set all Britain by the ears, because I unguardedly, rather under the temptation of being witty than disaffected, had declared my sentiments in favour of Parliamentary Reform, in the manner of that time, I was accused to the Board of Excise of being a Republican; and was very near being turned adrift in the wide world on that account. Mr Erskine of Mar, *a gentleman indeed*, wrote to my friend Glenriddell to know if I was really out of place on account of my political Principles; and if so, he proposed a Subscription among the friends of Liberty for me, which he offered to head, that I might be no pecuniary loser by my political integrity.

[Note by Burns accompanying a letter to John Francis Mar of Erskine, to whom, on 13 April 1793, he explained] – One of our Supervisors general, a Mr Corbet, was instructed to enquire, on the spot, into my conduct, and to document me 'that *my* business was to *act*, not to think; and that whatever might be Men or Measures, it was for me to be silent and obedient'. Between Mr Graham and him, I have been partially forgiven; only, I understand that all hopes of getting officially forward are blasted.

   to John Francis Erskine, 13 April 1793

Entre nous, you know my Politics; and I cannot approve of the honest Doctor's whining over the deserved fate of a certain pair of Personages [Louis XVI and Marie Antoinette]. What is there in the delivering over a perjured Blockhead and an unprincipled Prostitute to the hands of the hangman, that it should arrest for a moment, attention, in an eventful hour …

   to Mrs Dunlop, 20 December 1794

Portrait

Several people think that Allan's likeness of me is more striking than Naesmith's, for which I sat to him half-a-dozen times. However, there is an artist of very considerable merit just now in this town, who has hit the most remarkable likeness of what I am at this moment, that I think ever was taken of anybody. It is a small miniature … [by Miers]

> to George Thomson, May 1795

Poverty

Poverty! Thou half-sister of Death, thou cousin-german of Hell …

> to Peter Hill, 17 January 1791

Thou man of crazy care, and ceaseless sigh,
Still under bleak misfortune's blasting eye;
Doom'd to that sorest task of man alive –
To make three guineas do the work of five;
Laugh in misfortune's face, the beldam witch!
Say, you'll be merry – tho' you can't be rich.

> 'Occasional Address, Spoken by Miss Fontanelle, on her
> Benefit Night, 4 December 1793'

Pride

Strong pride of reasoning, with a little affectation of singularity, may mislead the best of hearts.

> to James Candlish, 21 March 1787

For my part, Madam, I trust I have too much pride for servility, and too little prudence for selfishness.

> to Mrs Dunlop, 15 April 1787

Thou fool, in thy phaeton towering,
    Art proud when that phaeton's praised?
'Tis the pride of a thief's exhibition
    When higher his pillory's raised.

> 'To the Honourable Mr R.M. – of P-m-e, on his high
> Phaeton'

O for a muse, not of heroic fire but satiric aquafortis, to
gnaw the iron pride of unfeeling greatness!

to Mrs Dunlop, January 1789

Printing

As to printing of Poetry, when you prepare it for the
Press, you have only to spell it right, and place the
capital letters properly; as to the punctuation, the
Printers do that themselves.

to Mrs Dunlop, November 1790

Prostitution

How is the fate of my poor Namesake Mademoiselle
Burns, decided? Which of their grave Lordships can lay
his hand on his heart and say that he has not taken
advantage of such frailty; nay, if we may judge by near
six thousand years experience, can the world do without
such frailty? ... As for those flinty-bosomed, puritanic
Prosecutors of Female Frailty ... may Woman curse
them! May Woman blast them! May Woman damn
them! May her lovely hand inexorably shut off the
Portal of Rapture to their most earnest Prayers and
fondest essays for entrance! And when many years and
much port and great business have delivered them over
to Vulture Gouts and Aspen Palsies, *then* may the dear
bewitching Charmer in derision throw open the blissful
Gate to tantalize their impotent desires which like ghosts
haunt their bosoms when all their powers to give or
receive enjoyment, are forever asleep in the sepulcre of
their fathers!!!

to Peter Hill, 2 February 1790

I give you credit for your sobriety with respect to that
universal vice, Bad Women. It is an impulse the hardest
to be restrained, but if once a man accustoms himself to

gratifications of that impulse, it is then nearly, or altogether impossible to restrain it. Whoring is a most ruinous expensive species of dissipation; is spending a poor fellow's money with which he ought to clothe and support himself nothing? Whoring has ninety-nine chances in a hundred to bring on a man the most nauseous and excruciating diseases to which human nature is liable; are disease and impaired constitution trifling considerations? All this independent of the criminality of it.

to William Burns, 10 February 1790

Prudence

Let prudence number o'er each sturdy son
Who life and wisdom at one race begun,
Who feel by reason and who give by rule,
(Instinct's a brute, and sentiment a fool!)
Who make poor, 'Will do' wait upon 'I should',
We own they're prudent – but who owns they're
    good?

'To Robert Graham of Fintry Esquire'

Quotation

I like to have quotations ready for every occasion. They give one's ideas so pat, and save one the trouble of finding expression adequate to one's feelings.

to Mrs Agnes M'Lehose, 14 January 1788

Do you know, I pick up favourite quotations, and store them in my mind as ready armour, offensive or defensive, amid the struggle of this turbulent existence.

to Mrs Dunlop, 6 December 1792

Let me quote you my two favourite passages, which, though I have repeated them ten thousand times, still they rouse my manhood and steel my resolution like inspiration.

On Reason build Resolve,
That column of true majesty in man.
[Edward] Young, 'Night Thoughts'

Hear, Alfred, hero of the state,
Thy genius heaven's high will declare;
The triumph of the truly great
Is never, never to despair!
Is never to despair!
[James Thomson] *Alfred: A Masque* (Act 1 Sce 3) to
Robert Ainslie, 6 January 1789

Rank

Princes and lords are but the breath o' kings,
   'An honest man's the noblest work of God:'
And *certes*, in fair Virtue's heavenly road,
   The *Cottage* leaves the *Palace* far behind.
What is a lordling's pomp? A cumbrous load,
   Disguising oft the *wretch* of human kind,
Studied in arts of Hell, in wickedness refin'd!
   'The Cottar's Saturday Night'

Ye see yon birkie ca'd a lord,
   Wha struts an' stares, an a' that;
Tho' hundreds worship at his word,
   He's but a coof for a' that;
For a' that, an' a' that,
   His ribband, star, an' a' that;
The man o' independent mind,
   He looks an' laughs at a' that …

A prince can mak a belted knight,
   A marquis, duke, and a' that;
But an honest man's aboon his might,
   Guid faith he mauna fa' that!

The rank is but the guinea's stamp;
    The man's the gowd for a' that.
  'For a' That an a' That'

If I'm design'd yon lordling's slave –
    By Nature's law designed –
Why was an independent wish
    E'er planted in my mind?
If not, why am I subject to
    His cruelty, or scorn?
Or why has Man the will and pow'r
    To make his fellow mourn?
  'Man was Made to Mourn – A Dirge'

Were this the charter of our state,
'On pain o' hell be rich an' great',
Damnation then would be our fate,
    Beyond remead;
But, thanks to heaven, that's no the gate
    We learn our creed.

For thus the royal mandate ran
When first the human race began;
'The social, friendly, honest man,
    Whate'er he be –
'Tis *he* fulfils great Nature's plan,
    And none but he.'
  'Second Epistle to John Lapraik'

Ye high, exalted virtuous dames,
    Tied up in godly laces,
Before ye gie poor Frailty names,
    Suppose a change o' cases.
A dear-lov'd lad, convenience snug
    A treach'rous inclination;

But, let me whisper i' your lug,
    Ye're aiblins nae temptation.
  'Address to the Unco Guid'

But gentlemen, an' ladies warst,
Wi' ev'n down want o' wark are curst.
They loiter, lounging, lank and lazy;
Tho' deil-haet ails them, yet uneasy;
Their days insipid, dull an' tasteless;
Their nights unquiet, lang and restless.
An' ev'n their sports, their balls an' races;
Their galloping through public places,
There's sic parade, sic pomp an' art,
The joy can scarcely reach the heart.
  'The Twa Dogs'

Your warlike Kings and Heroes bold,
    Great Captains and Commanders;
Your mighty Cèsars fam'd of old,
    And conquering Alexanders;
In fields they fought and laurels bought
    And bulwarks strong did batter,
But still they grac'd our noble list
    And ranked Fornicator!!!
  'The Fornicator: A New Song'

I sidling shelter'd in a neuk,
An' at his Lordship staw a leuk,
    Like some portentous omen;
Except good sense, an' social glee,
An' (what surprised me) modesty,
    I marked nought uncommon.

I watched the symptoms o' the great,
The gentle pride, the lordly state,

The arrogant assuming;
The fient a pride, nae pride had he,
Nor sauce, nor state, that I could see,
    Mair than an honest ploughman.
Then from his Lordship I shall learn,
Henceforth to meet with unconcern,
    One rank as well's another ...
    'Extemporare Verses on Dining with Lord Daer'

It requires no common exertion of good sense and philosophy in persons of elevated rank, to keep a friendship properly alive with one much their inferior.
    to Mrs Dunlop, 4 November 1787

The wailings of the rhyming tribe over the ashes of the Great, are damnably suspicious, and out of all character for sincerity.
    to Charles Hay, 24 December 1787

Why will Great people not only deafen us with the din of their equipage, and dazzle us with their fastidious pomp, but they must also be very dictatorially wise?
    to Mrs Agnes M'Lehose, 21 January 1788

It is so common with Poets when their Patrons try their hand at Rhyme, to cry up the Honourable or Right Honourable performance as Matchless, Divine, and etc., that I am afraid to open my mouth respecting your Poetic Extempores that you occasionally favour me with: I will only say you cannot oblige me more than sending them me.
    to Mrs Dunlop, 27 May 1788

What signify the silly, idle geegaws of wealth, or the ideal trumpery of greatness! When fellow-partakers of the same nature fear the same God, have the same benevolence of heart, the same nobleness of soul, the same detestation at everything dishonest, and the same scorn at everything unworthy – if they are not in the dependence of absolute beggary, in the name of common sense, are they not EQUALS?

to Margaret Chalmers, 16 September 1788

To crouch in the train of mere stupid wealth and greatness, except where the commercial interests of worldly prudence find their account in it, I hold to be prostitution in anyone that is not born a slave.

to Bruce Campbell, 13 November 1788

A man of consequence and fashion shall richly repay a deed of kindness with a nod and a smile, or a hearty shake of the hand; while a poor fellow labours under a sense of gratitude, which, like copper coin, though it loads the bearer, is yet of small account in the currency and commerce of the world.

to Henry Erskine, 22 January 1789

When I must skulk in a corner, lest the rattling equipage of some gaping blockhead, contemptible puppy, or detestable scoundrel should mangle me in the mire, I am tempted to exclaim – What merits these wretches had, or what demerit I have had, in some state of pre-existence, that they are ushered into this scene of being with the sceptre of rule and the key of riches in their puny fists, and I am kicked into the world, the sport of their folly, or the victim of their pride? ... Often, as I have glided through Princes Street, it has suggested itself to me as an improvement on the present human figure, that a man, in proportion to his own conceit of his consequence in the world, could have pushed out the longitude of his common size, as a snail pushes out its horns, or as we draw out a perspective. This trifling alteration, not to mention the prodigious saving, as it would be, in the wear and tear of the neck and limb of his Majesty's liege subjects in the way of tossing the head and tiptoe strutting, would evidently turn out a vast advantage in enabling us at once to adjust the ceremonials in making a bow or making way to a great Man, and that, too, within a second of the precise spherical angle of reverence, or an inch of the particular point of respectful distance, which the important creature itself requires; as a measuring-glance at its towering altitude would determine the affair like instinct.

> to Mrs Dunlop, 4 March 1789

How wretched is the man that hangs on and by the favours of the rich! To shrink from every dignity of Man at the approach of a lordly piece of self-consequence, who, amid all his tinsel glitter and stately hauteur, is but a creature formed as thou art ... came into the world as a puling infant as thou didst, and must go out of it as all men must, a stinking corpse – and should the important piece of clay-dough deign to rest his supercilious eye over you, and make a motion as if to signify his tremendous fiat – then – in all the quaking pangs and staring terrors of self-annihilation to stutter in crouching syllables 'Speak! Lord! for thy servant heareth!!!' If such is the damned state of the poor devil, from my soul I pity him!

> to Alexander Cunningham, 8 August 1789

When I pique myself on my independent spirit, I hope it is neither poetic licence, nor poetic rant; and I am so flattered with the honour you have done me, in making me your compeer in friendship and friendly corre-spondence, that I cannot without pain and a degree of mortification, be reminded of the real inequality between our situations.

to Mrs Dunlop, 25 January 1790

According to the hackneyed metaphor I value the several actors in the great drama of Life, simply as they perform their parts. I can look on a worthless fellow of a duke with unqualified contempt, and can regard an honest scavenger with sincere respect.

to Charles Sharpe, 22 April 1791

I remember in my plough-boy days, I could not conceive it possible that a noble lord could be a fool, or that a godly man could be a knave. How ignorant are plough-boys!

to Alexander Cunningham, 10 September 1792

I remember, and 'tis almost the earliest thing I do remember, when I was a young boy, one day at church, being enraged at seeing a young creature, one of the maids of the house, rise from the mouth of the pew to give way to a bloated son of wealth and dulness, who waddled surlily past her. Indeed, the girl was very pretty; and he was an ugly, stupid, purse-proud, money-loving old monster, as you can imagine.

to Miss Deborah Duff Davies, 6 April 1793

Does any man tell me, that my feeble efforts can be of no service; and that it does not belong to my humble station to meddle with the concerns of a people? I tell him, that it is on such individuals as I, that, for the hand of support and the eye of intelligence, a nation has to rest. The uninformed mob may swell a nation's bulk; and the titled, timid courtly throng may be its feathered ornament; but the number of those who are elevated

enough in life to reason and reflect; and yet low enough
to keep clear of the venal contagion of a Court; these are
a Nation's court.

>to John Francis Erskine of Mar (later 27 Earl of Mar and
>12th Lord Erskine), 13 April 1793

Religion

The cheerfu' supper done, wi' serious face,
>They, round the ingle, form a circle wide;
The Sire turns o'er, with patriarchal grace,
>The big ha'-Bible, ance his father's pride:
His bonnet rev'rently is laid aside,
>His lyart haffets wearing thin and bare;
Those strains that once did sweet in Zion glide,
>He wales a portion with judicious care;
And let us worship God! he says with solemn air.
>'The Cottar's Saturday Night'

Some books are lies frae end to end,
And some great lies are never penn'd:
Ev'n Ministers they have been kenn'd,
>In holy rapture,
A rousing whid at times to vend,
>And nail't wi' scripture.
>'Death and Dr Hornbrook'

Some quarrel the Presbyter gown,
>Some quarrel Episcopal graithing,
But every good fellow will own
>Their quarrel is all about naething …

The priest anathemas may threat,
>Predicament, Sir, that we're baith in;
But when honour's reveillé is beat,
>The holy artillery's naething.
>'Extemporare – to Gavin Hamilton'

King David o' poetic brief,
Wrought 'mang the lasses sic mischief
As fill'd his after life with grief
    An' bloody rants.
An' yet he's ranked amang the chief
     O' lang syne saunts.
  'Robert Burns' Answer (to Epistle from a Tailor)'

Learn three-mile pray'rs, an' half-mile graces,
Wi' weel-spread looves, an' lang, wry faces;
Grunt up a solemn, lengthen'd groan,
And damn a' parties but your own;
I'll warrant, then ye're nae deceiver,
A steady, sturdy, staunch believer.
  'A Dedication'

Orthodoxy! orthodoxy! who believes in John Knox,
    Let me sound an alarm to your conscience:
A heretic blast has been blown in the West,
    That 'what is no sense must be nonsense'.
  'The Kirk's Alarm'

An honest man may like a glass,
An honest man may like a lass,
But mean revenge, an' malice fause
    He'll still disdain,
An' then cry zeal for gospel laws,
    Like some we ken.
  'Epistle to the Reverend John M'Math'

But I gae mad at their grimaces,
Their sighin', cantin' grace-proud faces,
Their three-mile prayers, an' half-mile graces,
    Their raxin' conscience,
Whase greed, revenge, and pride disgraces
    Waur nor their nonsense …

God knows, I'm no the thing I should be,
Nor am I even the thing I cou'd be,
But twenty times I rather would be
    An atheist clean,
Than under gospel colours hid be
    Just for a screen ...
    'To the Reverend John M'Math'

What a poor, pimping business is a Presbyterian place of
worship, dirty, narrow and squalid, stuck in a corner of
old Popish grandeur such as Linlithgow and, much
more, Melrose! Ceremony and show, if judiciously
thrown in, absolutely necessary for the bulk of mankind,
both in religious and civil matters.
    Journal of the Highland Tour, 25 August 1787

An honest man has nothing to fear. If we lie down in the
grave, the whole man a piece of broke machinery, to
moulder with the clods of the valley – be it so; at least
there is an end of pain, care, woes and wants; if that part
of us called Mind does survive the apparent destruction
of the man – away with old-wife prejudices and tales!
Every age and nation has had a different set of stories;
and as the many are always weak, of consequence they
have often, perhaps always been deceived. A man,
conscious of having acted an honest part among his
fellow-creatures; even granting that he may have been
the sport, at times, of passions and instincts; he goes to a
great unknown Being who could have no other end in
giving him existence but to make him happy; who gave
him those passions and instincts, and well knows their
force.
    to Robert Muir, 7 March 1788

I have every possible reverence for the much-talk'd-of world beyond the Grave, and I wish that which Piety believes and Virtue deserves may be all matter of fact; but in all things belonging to, and terminating in, this present Scene of Existence, man has serious and interesting business on hand.

to Robert Ainslie, 30 June 1788

I am in perpetual warfare with that doctrine of our Reverend Priesthood, that 'we are born into this world bond slaves of iniquity and heirs of perdition, wholly inclined' to that which is evil and wholly disinclined to that which is good, until by a kind of Spiritual Filtration or rectifying process called effectual Calling etc. The whole business is reversed, and our connections above and below completely change place. I believe in my conscience that the case is just quite contrary. We come into the world with a heart and disposition to do good for it, until by dashing a large mixture of base Alloy called Prudence, alias Selfishness, the too precious Metal of the Soul is brought down to the blackguard Sterling of ordinary currency.

to Miss Rachael Dunlop, 2 August 1788

I had an old Grand-uncle, with whom my Mother lived a while in her girlish years; the good, old man, for such he was, was long blind ere he died, during which time his most voluptuous enjoyment was to sit down and cry, while my Mother would sing the simple old song of The Life and Age of Man.

It is this way of thinking, it is these melancholy truths, that make Religion so precious to the poor miserable Children of men. If it is a mere phantasm, existing only in the heated imagination of Enthusiasm.

'What truth on earth so precious as the Lie!' [Young:

Night Thoughts]. My idle reasonings sometimes make
me a little sceptical, but the necessities of my heart
always give the cold philosophisings the lie.

to Mrs Dunlop, 16 August 1788

Mine is the Religion of the bosom. I hate the very idea of
controversial divinity; as I firmly believe, that every
honest, upright man, of whatever sect, will be accepted
by the Deity.

to Mrs M'Lehose, 12 December 1788

I never heard the loud, solitary whistle of the Curlew in
a Summer noon, or the wild, mixing cadence of a troop
of grey plover in an Autumnal morning, without feeling
an elevation of Devotion or Poesy. Tell me, my dear
Friend, to what can this be owing? Are we a piece of
machinery, which, like the Eolian harp, passive, takes
the impression of the passing accident? Or do these
workings argue something within us above the trodden
clod?

to Mrs Dunlop, 1 January 1789

My creed is pretty nearly expressed in the last clause of
Jamie Deans's grace, an honest weaver in Ayrshire:
'Lord, grant that we may lead a gude life for a gude life
maks a gude end; at least it helps weel!'

to Mrs Agnes M'Lehose, 8 January 1788

That there is an incomprehensible Great Being, to whom
I owe my existence; and that He must be intimately
acquainted with the operations and progress of the
internal   machinery,   and   consequent   outward
deportment, of this creature which He has made; these
are, I think, self-evident propositions. That there is a real
and eternal distinction between virtue and vice, and,

consequently, that I am an accountable creature; that from the seeming nature of the human mind, as well as from the evident imperfection, nay, positive injustice, in the administration of affairs both in the natural and moral worlds, there must be a retributive scene of existence beyond the grave; must, I think, be allowed by everyone who will give himself a moment's reflection.

to Mrs Dunlop, 21 June 1789

We are all equally creatures of some Great Creator; and among the many enormous instances of capricious partiality in the Administration of this world which cry to Heaven for retribution and vengeance in some other state of existence, I think it is none of the least flagrant, that power which one creature of us has to amuse himself by and at the expense of another's misery, torture and death.

to Patrick Miller, 21 June 1789

Whatever mitigates the woes, or increases the happiness, of others, this is my criterion of goodness; and whatever injures society at large, or any individual in it, this is my measure of iniquity.

to Mrs Dunlop, 21 June 1789

An honest candid enquirer after truth I revere; but illiberality and wrangling I equally detest.

to Mrs Dunlop, 17 July 1789

Religion, my dear friend, is the true comfort! A strong persuasion in a future state of existence; a proposition so obviously probable, that, setting revelation aside, every nation and people, so far as investigation has reached, for at least near four thousand years, have, in some mode or other, firmly believed it. In vain would we reason and pretend to doubt. I have myself done so to a very daring pitch; but when I reflected, that I was opposing the most ardent wishes and the most darling hopes of good men, and flying in the face of all human belief, in all ages, I was shocked at my own conduct.

to Mrs Dunlop, 6 September 1789

Jesus Christ, thou amiablest of characters, I trust thou art no Impostor, and that thy revelation of blissful scenes of existence beyond death and the grave, is not one of the many impositions which time after time have been palmed on credulous mankind.

to Mrs Dunlop, 13 December 1789

God grant that there be another world more congenial to honest fellows, beyond this. A world where these rubs and plagues of absence, distance, misfortunes, ill-health, etc., shall no more damp hilarity and divide friendship.

to William Dunbar, 14 January 1790

All my fears and cares are of this world: if there is Another, an honest man has nothing to fear from it. I hate a man that wishes to be a Deist, but I fear, every fair, unprejudiced Enquirer must in some degree be a Sceptic ... One thing frightens me much: that we are to live forever, seems too good news to be true. That we are to enter into a new scene of existence, where exempt from want and pain we shall enjoy ourselves and our friends without satiety or separation – how much would I be indebted to anyone who could fully assure me that this was certain fact!

to Alexander Cunningham, 16 February 1790

I hope, and believe, that there is a state of existence beyond the grave where the worthy of this life will renew their former intimacies ... Still the damned dogmas of reasoning Philosophy throw in their doubts; but upon the whole, I believe, or rather I have a kind of conviction, though not absolute certainty, of the world beyond the grave.

to Mrs Dunlop, 22 August 1792

Of all Nonsense, Religious Nonsense is the most nonsensical.

to Alexander Cunningham, 10 September 1792

Can you tell me, my dear Cunningham, why a religious turn of mind has always a tendency to narrow and illiberalise the heart?

to Alexander Cunningham, 10 September 1792

There are two great pillars that bear us up, amid the wreck of misfortune and misery. The one is composed of the different modifications of a certain noble, stubborn something in man, known by the name of courage, fortitude, magnanimity. The other is made up of those feelings and sentiments which, however the sceptic may deny them or the enthusiast disfigure them, are yet, I am convinced, original and component parts of the human soul; those *senses of the mind*, if I may be allowed the expression, which connect us with, and link us to, those awful obscure realities – an all-powerful and equally beneficent God, and a world to come, beyond death and the grave. The first gives the nerve of combat, while a ray of hope beams on the field; the last pours the balm of comfort into the wound which time can never cure.

to Alexander Cunningham, 25 February 1794

Remorse

Many and sharp the num'rous ills
    Inwoven with our frame!
More pointed still we make ourselves,
    Regret, Remorse and Shame!
  'Man was Made to Mourn'

I entirely agree with that judicious philosopher Mr Smith in his excellent theory of Moral Sentiments, that Remorse is the most painful sentiment that can embitter the human bosom.

  First Commonplace Book, September 1783

Clarinda, my life, you have wounded my soul ... If in the moment of fond endearment and tender dalliance, I perhaps trespassed against the *letter* of Decorum's law; I appeal, even to you, whether I ever sinned in the very least degree against the *spirit* of her strictest statute.

  to Mrs Agnes M'Lehose, 25 January 1788

Can you minister to a mind diseased? Can you, amid the horrors of penitence, regret, remorse, headache, nausea, and all the rest of the d—d hounds of hell that beset a poor wretch who has been guilty of the sin of drunkenness – can you speak peace to a troubled soul?

  to Robert Ainslie, *c.* November 1791

I believe last night that my old enemy, the Devil, taking the advantage of my being in drink ... tempted me to be a little turbulent. You have too much humanity to heed the maniac ravings of a poor wretch whom the powers of Hell, and the potency of Port, beset at the same time.

  to John M'Murdo, 1792

I daresay this is the first epistle you ever received from the nether world. I write to you from the regions of Hell, amid the horrors of the damned ... O all ye powers of decency and decorum! whisper ... that my errors, though great, were involuntary – that an intoxicated man is the vilest of beasts ... that to be rude to a woman, when in my senses, was impossible to me – but

*　*　*

Regret! Remorse! Shame! ye three hellhounds that ever dog my steps and bay at my heels, spare me!
　　　to Mrs Maria Riddell, December 1793

In a face where I used to meet the kind complacency of friendly confidence, *now* to find cold neglect and contemptuous scorn – is a wrench that my heart can ill bear. It is, however, some kind of miserable good luck; that while De-haut-en-bas rigour may depress an unoffending wretch to the ground, it has a tendency to rouse a stubborn something in his bosom, which, though it cannot heal the wounds of the soul, is at least an opiate to blunt their poignancy.
　　　to Mrs Maria Riddell, 12 January 1794

I was, I know, drunk last night, but I am sober this morning. From the expressions Captain Dods made use of to me, had I had nobody's welfare to care for but my own, we should certainly have come, according to the manners of the world, to the necessity of murdering one another about the business. The words were such as generally, I believe, end in a brace of pistols; but I still am pleased to think, that I did not ruin the peace and welfare of a family of children in a drunken squabble. Farther, you know that the report of certain Political opinions being mine, has already once before brought me to the brink of destruction. I dread lest last night's business may be misrepresented in the same way. YOU,

I beg, will take care to prevent it. I tax your wish for Mrs Burns's welfare with the task of waiting as soon as possible, on every gentleman who was present, and state this to him, and as you please, show him this letter. What after all was the obnoxious toast? 'May our success in the present war be equal to the justice of our cause' a toast that the most outrageous frenzy of loyalty cannot object to. I request and beg that this morning you will wait on the parties present at the foolish dispute. The least delay may be of unlucky consequence to me.

to Samuel Clarke, July 1794

Rivers

Ayr gurgling kissed his pebbled shore,
O'erhung with wild-woods, thick'ning green;
The fragrant birch, and hawthorn hoar,
Twined, am'rous, round the raptured scene:
The flowers sprang wanton to be prest,
The birds sang love on ev'ry spray;
Till too, too soon the glowing west
Proclaimed the speed of winged day.
'Thou Lingering Star'

When heavy, dark, continued, a'-day rains
Wi' deepening deluges o'erflow the plains;
When from the hills where springs the brawling Coil,
Or stately Lugar's messy fountains boil;
Or where the Greenock winds his moorland course,
Or haunted Garpal draws his feeble source,
Arous'd by blustering winds an' spotting thowes,
In many a torrent down the snaw-broo rowes,
While crushing ice, borne on the roaring spate,
Sweeps dawns, an' mills, an' brigs, a' to the gate!
Auld Ayr is just one lengthen'd, tumbling sea.
'The Brigs of Ayr'

One night as I did wander,
    When corn begins to shoot,
I sat me down to ponder,
    Upon an old tree root;
Auld Ayr ran by before me,
    And bicker'd to the seas;
A cushat crooded o'er me,
    That echoed through the braes.
  'A Fragment'

Here, foaming down the skelvy rocks,
    In twisting strength I rin:
There, high my boiling torrent smokes,
    Wild-roaring o'er a linn:
Enjoying large each spring and well,
    As Nature gave them me,
I am, altho' I say't myself,
    Worth gaun a mile to see.
  'The Humble Petition of Bruar Water'

The braes ascend like lofty wa's,
The foamy stream deep-roaring fa's,
O'erhung wi' fragrant-spreading shaws –
    The birks o' Aberfeldy.
  'The Birks o' Aberfeldy'

How pleasant the banks of the clear-winding Devon,
With green-spreading bushes and flowers blooming
      fair!
  'The Banks of Devon'

Streams that glide in orient plains,
Never bound by Winter's chains;
Glowing here on golden sands,
There immixed with foulest stains

From Tyranny's empurpled hands:
These, their richly gleaming waves,
I leave to tyrants and their slaves;
Give me the stream that sweetly laves
   The banks by Castle Gordon.
   'Castle Gordon'

Amang the bonnie winding banks,
    Where Doon rins, wimplin' clear;
Where Bruce ance ruled the martial ranks,
    An' shook his Carrick spear;
Some merry, friendly, country-folks
    Together did convene,
To burn their nits, an' pou their stocks,
    An' haud their Hallowe'en.
   'Hallowe'en'

Flow gently, sweet Afton, among thy green braes,
Flow gently, I'll sing thee a song in thy praise;
My Mary's asleep by thy murmuring stream,
Flow gently, sweet Afton, disturb not her dream.
   'Flow Gently, Sweet Afton'

Scholars

His lockèd, lettered, braw brass collar,
Shew'd him the gentleman an' scholar.
   'The Twa Dogs'

What's a' your jargon o' your schools –
Your Latin names for horns and stools?
If honest Nature made you fools,
    What sairs your grammars?
Ye'd better turn up spades and shools
    Or knappin-hammers.

A set o' dull, conceited hashes
Confuse their brains in college-classes!
They gang in stirks, and come out asses,
    Plain truth to speak;
An' syne they think to climb Parnassus
    By dint o' Greek!

Gie me ae spark o' Nature's fire,
That's a' the learning I desire;
Then tho' I drudge thro' dub an' mire
    At pleugh or cart,
My Muse, tho' hamely in attire,
    May touch the heart.
  'Epistle to John Lapraik'

Scotland

O Scotia! my dear, my native soil!
    For whom my warmest wish to Heaven is sent!
Long may thy hardy sons of rustic toil
    Be blest with health, and peace, and sweet
      content!
And O! may Heaven their simple lives prevent
    From luxury's contagion, man and wife!
Then, howe'er crowns and coronets be rent,
    A virtuous Populace may rise the while,
And stand, a wall of fire, around their much-lov'd
    isle.
  'The Cottar's Saturday Night'

I wish for nothing more than to make a leisurely
Pilgrimage through my native country; to sit and muse
on those once hard-contended fields, where Caledonia,
rejoicing, saw her bloody lion borne through broken
ranks to victory and fame; and catching the inspiration,
to pour the deathless Names in Song.
    to the Earl of Buchan, 7 February 1787

This morning I knelt at the tomb of Sir John the Graham, the gallant friend of the immortal Wallace; and two hours ago I said a fervent prayer for Old Caledonia over the hole in a blue whinstone, where Robert de Bruce fixed his royal standard on the banks of Bannockburn; and just now, from Stirling Castle, I have seen by the setting sun the glorious prospect of the windings of Forth through the rich carse of Stirling ...
    to Robert Muir, 26 August 1787

Thus bold, independent, unconquer'd and free,
    Her bright course of glory for ever shall run;
For brave Caledonia immortal must be,
    I'll prove it from Euclid as clear as the sun:
Rectangle-triangle the figure we'll choose,
    The upright is Chance, and old Time is the base;
But brave Caledonia's the Hypothenuse,
    Then, Ergo, she'll match them, and match them
        always.
    'Caledonia'

Here, Land o' Cakes, and brither Scots,
Frae Maidenkirk to John o' Groats,
If there's a hole in a' your coats,
    I rede you tent it:
A chield's amang you, takin' notes,
    And, faith, he'll prent it.
    'On the late Captain Grose's Peregrinations through
        Scotland'

Auld Scotland has a raucle tongue;
She's just a devil wi' a rung;
An' if she promise auld or young
    To tak their part,

169

Tho' by the neck she should be strung
   She'll no desert.
   'The Author's Earnest Cry and Prayer'

The only things that are to be found in this country, in any degree of perfection, are Stupidity and Canting. Prose they only know in graces, prayers etc., and the value of these they estimate, as they do their plaiding webs – by the Ell; as for the Muses, they have as much idea of a Rhinocerous as a Poet.
   to John Beugo, 9 September 1788

Scots song

The world may think slightingly of the craft of song-making if they please, but, as Job says – 'O that mine adversary had written a book' – let them try. There is a certain something in the Old Scotch songs, a wild happiness of thought and expression, which peculiarly marks them, not only from English songs, but also from the modern efforts of song-wrights, in our native manner and language … An engraver in this town has set about collecting and publishing all the Scotch songs, with the music, that can be found. Songs in the English language, if by Scotchmen, are admitted, but the music must all be Scotch. Drs Beattie and Blacklock are lending a hand, and the first musician in town presides over that department. I have been absolutely crazed about it, collecting old stanzas, and every information remaining respecting their origins, authors, and etc., and etc.
   to the Reverend John Skinner, 25 October 1787

I have scarcely made a single distich since I saw you. When I meet with an old Scots air that has any facetious idea in its name, I have a peculiar pleasure in following out that idea for a verse or two.
   to William Dunbar, 7 April 1788

I have just this moment got your letter. As the request you make to me will positively add to my enjoyments in complying with it, I shall enter into your undertaking with all the small portion of abilities I have, strained to their utmost exertions by the impulse of Enthusiasm ... As to my remuneration, you may think my Songs either *above* or *below* price ... In the honest enthusiasm with which I embark in your undertaking, to talk of money, wages, fee, hire, and etc., would be downright sodomy of soul.

to George Thomson, 16 September 1792

The Songs in the second Volume of the Museum marked D, are Dr Blacklock's; but as I am sorry to say they are far short of his other works ... Those marked T, are the work of an obscure, tippling but extraordinary body by the name of Tytler: a mortal, who though he drudges about Edinburgh as a common Printer, with leaky shoes, a sky-lighted hat and knee buckles as unlike George-by-the-grace-of-God and Solomon-the-son-of-David, yet that unknown drunken Mortal is Author and compiler of three fourths of Elliot's pompous Encylopedia Brittanica. Those marked Z I have given to the world as old verses to their respective tunes; but in fact, of a good many of them, little more than the Chorus is ancient ...

to Mrs Dunlop, 13 November 1788

Perhaps you may not find your account, *lucratively*, in this business, but you are a Patriot for the Music of your Country; and I am certain, Posterity will look on themselves as highly indebted to your Public spirit.

to James Johnson, 15 November 1788

'Laddie, lie near me' – must *lie by me*, for some time. I do not know the air; and until I am complete master of a tune, in my own singing (such as it is) I never can compose for it. My way is: I consider the poetic Sentiment, correspondent to my idea of the musical expression; then chuse my theme; begin one Stanza; when that is composed, which is generally the most difficult part of the business, I walk out, sit down and then, look out for objects in Nature around me that are in unison or harmony with the cogitations of my fancy and workings of my bosom; humming every now and then the air with the verses I have framed; when I feel my Muse beginning to jade, I retire to the solitary fireside of my study, and there, on the hind-legs of my elbow-chair, by way of calling forth my own critical strictures, as my pen goes – Seriously, this, at home, is almost always invariably my way. What dam'd egotism!

to George Thomson, September 1793

One song more and I have done – Auld lang syne ... the old song of the olden times, and which has never been in print, nor even in manuscript, until I took it down from an old man's singing.

to George Thomson, September 1793

I have not that command of the language that I have of my native tongue. In fact, I think my ideas are more barren in English than in Scots.

to George Thomson, 1 April 1794

Give me leave to criticise your taste in the only thing in which it is in my opinion reprehensible; (you know I ought to know something of my own trade) of pathos, Sentiment, and Point, you are a complete judge; but there is a quality more necessary than either in Song, and which is the very essence of a Ballad, I mean Simplicity. Now, if I mistake not, this last feature you are a little apt to sacrifice to the foregoing.

to George Thomson, April 1793

A small sprinkling of Scoticisms is no objection to an English reader.

> to George Thomson, September 1793

Self-pity

Time cannot aid me, my griefs are immortal,
Nor hope dare a comfort bestow;
Come then, enamour'd and fond of my anguish,
Enjoyment I'll seek in my woe.

> 'Fair Jenny'

Sex

In Edinburgh town they've made a law,
In Edinburgh at the Court o' Session,
That standing pricks are fauteors a',
And guilty of a high transgression ...

And they've provided dungeons deep,
Ilk lass has ane in her possession;
Until the wretches wail and weep,
They there shall lie for their transgression.

> 'Act Sederunt of the Session, A Scots Ballad'

I maun hae a wife, whatso'er she be;
An she be a woman, that's enough for me.

If that she be bony, I shall think her right;
If that she be ugly, where's the odds at night?

> 'A Broom Besoms'

Lo worms enjoy the seat of bliss
Where Lords and Lairds afore did kiss.

> Epitaph

Like to a fading flower in May,
    Which gardener cannot save,
So Beauty must, sometimes, decay
    And drop into the grave.

Fair Burns, for long the talk and toast
    Of many a gaudy Beau,
That Beauty has forever lost
    That made each bosom glow …

Beneath this cold, green sod lies dead
    That once bewitching dame
That freed Edina's lustful sons,
    And quench'd their glowing flame.
    'To the Memory of the Unfortunate Miss Burns, 1791'

O steer her up and be na blate,
    An' gin she tak it ill, jo,
Then lea the lassie till her fate,
    And time nae langer spill, jo:
Ne'er break your heart for ae rebuke,
    But think upon it still, jo,
That gin the lassie winna do't,
    Ye'll fin' another will, jo.
    'O Steer Her up and Haud her Gaun'

What can a young lassie, what shall a young lassie,
What can a young lassie do wi' an auld man?
    'What Can a Young Lassie Do wi' an Auld Man?'

Lament him, Mauchline husbands a',
    He aften did assist ye;
For had ye stayed whole weeks awa,
    Your wives they ne'er had missed ye.

Ye Mauchline bairns, as on ye pass
    To school in bands thegither,
O tread ye lightly on his grass;
    Perhaps he was your father.
  'On a Wag in Mauchline'

O, I hae tint my rosy cheek,
    Likewise my waist sae sma';
O wae gae by the sodger lown,
    The sodger did it a' ...

Now I maun thole the scornfu' sneer
    O mony a saucy quine;
When, curse upon her godly face!
    Her c—t's as merry's mine.

Our dame hauds up her wanton tail,
    As due as she doun lie;
And yet misca's a young thing
    The trade if she but try.
  'The Merry Muses of Caledonia'

I once was a maid, tho' I canna tell when,
And still my delight is in proper young men;
Some one of a troop of dragoons was my daddie,
No wonder I'm fond of a sodger laddie.
  'The Jolly Beggars'

Rosebery to his lady says,
    'My hinnie and my succour,
O shall we do the thing ye ken,
    Or shall we take our supper?'

Wi' modest face, sae fu' o' grace,
    Replied the bonny lady;

'My noble lord do as you please,
 But supper is na ready' …
 'The Merry Muses of Caledonia'

The night it was a haly night,
 The day had been a haly day;
Kilmarnock gleam'd wi' candle light,
 As Girzie hameward took her way.
A man o' sin, ill may he thrive!
 And never haly meetings see!
Wi' godly Girzie met belye,
 Amang the Craigie hills sae hie.

The chiel was wight, the chiel was stark,
 He had na wait to chap or ca',
And she was faint wi' haly wark,
 She had na pith to say him na.
But ay she glowr'd up to the moon
 And ay she sigh'd most piteously;
'I trust my heart's in heaven aboon,
 Whare'er your sinfu' pintle be.'
 'The Merry Muses of Caledonia'

Some cry, Constitution!
 Some cry, Revolution!
And Politics kick up a rowe;
 But Prince and Republic,
 Agree on the subject,
No treason is in a good mowe.
 'A Ballad'

O, what a peacemaker is a guid weel-willy pintle! It is
the mediator, the guarantee, the umpire, the bond of
union, the solemn league and covenant, the plenipoten-
tiary, the Aaron's rod, the Jacob's staff, the prophet

Elisha's pot of oil, the Ahasuerus' sceptre, the sword of mercy, the philosopher's stone, the horn of plenty, and Tree of Life between Man and Woman.

> to Robert Ainslie, 3 March 1788

Sin

I confess I have sinned for which there is hardly any forgiveness, ingratitude to Friendship, in not writing you sooner ...

> to William Chalmers, 27 December 1786

Though I am not without my fears respecting my fate, at that grand, universal inquest of right and wrong commonly called *The Last Day*, yet I trust there is one sin, which that arch-vagabond, Satan ... cannot throw in my teeth. I mean ingratitude. There is a certain pretty large quantum of kindness for which I remain, and from inability, I fear must still remain, your debtor; but though unable to repay the debt, I assure you, Sir, I shall ever warmly remember the obligation.

> to John M'Auley, 4 June 1789

O Lord! yestreen, Thou kens, wi' Meg –
Thy pardon I sincerely beg –
O, may't ne'er be a living plague
    To my dishonour!
An' I'll ne'er lift a lawless leg
    Again upon her.
> 'Holy Willie's Prayer'

Sport

Avaunt, away! the cruel sway,
    Tyrannic man's dominion;
The sportsman's joy, the murd'ring cry,
    The fluttering, gory pinion!
> 'Now Westlin' Winds'

Thoughts

Thoughts that are the spontaneous result of accidental situations, either respecting health, place, or company, have often a strength, and always an originality, that would in vain be looked for in fancied circumstances and studied paragraphs.

to Mrs Dunlop, 10 August 1788

Time

Time is too short for ceremonies.

to Mrs Agnes M'Lehose, 12 December 1787

War

O wae upon you, Men o' State,
That brethern rouse in deadly hate!
As ye make mony a fond heart mourn,
Sae may it on your heads return!
'O Logan Sweetly dost Thou Glide'

Ye hypocrites! are these your pranks?
To murder men, and gie God thanks?
Desist, for shame! – proceed no further
God won't accept your thanks for MURTHER!
'Thanksgiving for a National Victory'

In the field of proud honour, our swords in our
hands,
Our King and our Country to save;
While victory shines on life's last ebbing sands,
O who would not die with the Brave?
'The Song of Death'

Let other heroes boast their scars,
　　The marks of sturt and strife;
And other poets sing of wars,
　　The plagues of human life.
Shame fa' the fun; wi' sword and gun
　　To slap mankind like lumber!
I sing his name, and nobler fame,
　　Wha multiplies our number.
　'Nature's Law'

I murder hate by field or flood,
　　Tho' glory's name may screen us;
In wars at home I'll spend my blood –
　　Life-giving wars of Venus.

The deities that I adore
　　Are social Peace and Plenty;
I'm better pleased to make one more
　　Than be the death of twenty.
　'I Murder Hate'

Wealth
The warld's wealth, when I think on,
　　Its pride and a' the lave o't;
O fie on silly coward man
　　That he should be the slave o't.
　'Poortith Cauld and Restless Love'

Weather
As to your cold, you are so accustomed to, so hardened
by our villainous climate, that I hope you will soon get
the better of your complaint.
　　to Mrs Dunlop, 24 September 1792

The lazy mist hangs from the brow of the hill …
  'The Fall of the Leaf'

While at the stook the shearers cow'r
To shun the bitter blaudin show'r
Or in gulravage rinnin' scow'r
    To pass the time,
To you I dedicate this hour
    In idle rhyme.
  'Epistle to the Reverend John M'Math'

Ae hairst afore the Sherra-moor,
    I mind't as weel's yestreen –
I was a gilpey then, I'm sure
    I was na past fyfteen:
The simmer had been cauld and wat,
    An' stuff was unco green.
  'Hallowe'en'

November chill blaws loud wi' angry sugh;
    The short'ning winter-day is near a close,
The miry beasts retreating frae their pleugh;
    The black'ning trains o' craws to their repose.
  'The Cottar's Saturday Night'

Last day my mind was in a bog,
    Down George's street I stoited;
A creeping, cauld prosaic fog
    My vera senses doited.
  'To Miss Ferrier'

May Boreas ne'er thresh your rigs,
Nor kick your rickles aff their legs,
Sendin' the stuff o'er muirs and haggs
    Like drivin' wrack;

But may the tapmost grain that wags
　　Come to the sack.
　'Third Epistle to John Lapraik'

When lyart leaves bestrow the yird,
Or wavering like the bauckie-bird,
　　Bedim cauld Boreas' blast;
When hailstanes drive wi' bitter skyte,
And infant frosts begin to bite,
　　In hoary crancreuch drest,
Ae night at e'en a merry core
　　O' randie, gangrel bodies,
In Poosie-Nansie's held the splore
　　To drink their orra duddies …
　'The Jolly Beggars'

Come winter, with thine angry howl,
　　And raging, bend the naked tree;
Thy gloom will soothe my cheerless soul,
　　When Nature all is sad like me!
　'And Maun I Still on Menie Doat'

Ev'n winter bleak has charms to me,
When winds rave thro' the naked tree;
Or frost on hills of Ochiltree
　　Are heavy gray;
Or blinding drifts wild-furious flee,
　　Dark'ning the day!
　'Epistle to William Simson'

Blow, blow, ye winds, with heavier gust!
And freeze, thou bitter-biting frost!
Descend, ye chilly, smothering snows!
Not all your rage, as now united shows
　　More hard unkindness, unrelenting,
　　Vengeful malice, unrepenting,

Than heaven-illumined Man on brother Man
      bestows.
  'A Winter Night'

Cauld blaws the wind frae east to west,
    The drift is drifting sairly;
Sae loud and shrill I hear the blast,
    I'm sure it's winter fairly.

Up in the mornin's no for me,
    Up in the morning early;
When a' the hills are cover'd in snaw,
    I'm sure it's winter fairly.
  'Up in the Morning Early'

This morning I had set apart for a visit to my honoured
friend ... when behold, 'the snows descended, and the
winds blew', and made my journey impracticable.
    to Mrs Dunlop, January 1789

A storm naturally overblows itself.
    to John Arnot of Dalquwhatswood, April 1786

Woman

There's nought but care on ev'ry han',
    In ev'ry hour that passes, O;
What signifies the life o' man,
    An' twerena for the lasses, O ...

Auld nature swears, the lovely dears
    Her noblest work she classes O;
Her prentice han' she tried on man,
    An' then she made the lasses O.
  'Green Grow the Rashes'

But Woman, Nature's darling child,
    There all her charms she does compile,
And all her other works are foil'd
    By th' bony lass o' Ballochmyle.
  'On Miss W.A.'

Hale to the sex, ilk gude chiel says,
Wi' merry dance in winter-days,
    An' we to share in common:
The gust o' joy, tha balm of woe,
The saul o' life, the heav'n below,
    Is rapture-giving woman.
  'The Answer'
  (to the Guidwife of Wauchope House)

Of a' the airts the wind can blaw,
    I dearly like the west;
For there the bony Lassie lives,
    The Lassie I lo'e best:
There's wild woods grow, and rivers row,
    And mony a hill between;
But day and night, my fancy's flight
    Is ever wi' my Jean.

I see her in the dewy flowers,
    I see her sweet and fair;
I hear her in the tunefu' birds,
    I hear her charm the air;
There's not a bony flower that springs
    By fountain, shaw, or green;
There's not a bony bird that sings
    But minds me o' my Jean.
  'I Love my Jean'

A bonnie lass, I will confess,
    Is pleasant to the e'e:
But without some better qualities,
    She's no a lass for me ...

A gaudy dress and gentle air
    May slightly touch the heart;
But it's innocence and modesty
    That polishes the dart.
  'Handsome Nell'

There lives a lass beyond yon park,
I'd rather have her in her sark,
Than you wi' a' your thousand mark;
    That gars you look so high.
  'Tibbie, I hae Seen the Day'

O wha my babie-clouts will buy?
O wha will tent me when I cry?
Wha will kiss me where I lie?
The rantin' dog the daddie o't.
  'The Rantin' Dog the Daddie O't'

Great love I bear to all the Fair,
    Their humble slave an' a' that;
But lordly Will, I hold it still
    A mortal sin to thraw that ...
Their tricks an' craft hae put me daft,
    They've taen me in, an' a' that;
But clear your decks, an' here's the Sex!
    I like the jads for a' that.
  'The Jolly Beggars'

Yestreen when to the trembling string
    The dance gaed through the lighted ha',
To thee my fancy took its wing,
    I sat, but neither heard, nor saw:
Though this was fair, and that was braw,
    And yon the toast of a' the town,
I sighed, and said amang them a',
    'Ye are na Mary Morison.'
  'Mary Morison'

My heart is sair, I dare na tell,
    My heart is sair for Somebody;
I could wake a winter-night
    For the sake o' Somebody.
  'For the Sake o' Somebody'

Will ye go the Highlands, Leezie Lindsay,
    Will ye go to the Highlands wi' me;
Will ye go to the Highlands, Leezie Lindsay
    My pride and my darling to be?
  'Leezie Lindsay'

My love she's but a lassie yet,
    My love she's but a lassie yet;
We'll let her stand a year or twa,
    She'll no be half sae saucy yet.
  'My Love She's but a Lassie Yet'

I'm o'er young, I'm o'er young,
    I'm o'er young to marry yet;
I'm o'er young, 'twad be a sin
    To tak me frae my mammy yet.
  'I'm o'er Young to Marry Yet'

View the wither'd beldam's face –
Can thy keen inspection trace
Aught of Humanity's sweet, melting grace?
Note that eye, 'Tis rheum o'erflows,
Pity's flood there never rose.
See those hands, ne'er stretched to save,
Hands that took – but never gave.
Keeper of Mammon's iron chest,
Lo, there she goes, unpitied and unblest,
She goes, but not to realms of everlasting rest!
   'Ode, Sacred to the Memory of Mrs Oswald of
         Auchencruive'

And I will pu' the pink, the emblem o' my dear,
For she's the pink o' womankind, and blooms
        without a peer ...
   'The Posie'

I hae been blythe wi' Comrades dear;
   I hae been merry drinking;
I hae been joyfu' gathering gear;
   I hae been happy thinking;
But a' the pleasures e'er I saw,
   Tho' three times doubled fairly –
That happy night was worth them a',
    Amang the rigs o' barley.
      Corn rigs, an' barley rigs,
       An' corn rigs are bonie;
      I'll ne'er forget that happy night,
       Amang the rigs wi' Annie.
   'Corn Rigs are Bonie'

Surely woman, amiable woman, is often made in vain!
Too delicately formed for the rougher pursuits of
ambition; too noble for the dirt of avarice, and even too

gentle for the rage of pleasure: formed indeed for and highly susceptible of enjoyment and rapture; but that enjoyment, alas! almost wholly at the mercy of the caprice, malevolence, stupidity, or wickedness of an animal at all times comparatively unfeeling, and often brutal ...

to Margaret Chalmers, 14 March 1788

Women have a kind of sturdy sufferance which qualifies them to endure beyond, much beyond the common run of Men; but perhaps part of that fortitude is owing to their short-sightedness, as they are by no means famous for seeing remote consequences in all their real importance.

to William Burns, 10 November 1789

Bewitching Poesy is like bewitching WOMAN; she has in all ages been accused of misleading Mankind from the counsels of Wisdom and the paths of Prudence; involving them in Infamy, and plunging them in the vortex of Ruin; yet where is the Man but must own, that all our happiness on earth is not worthy the name! that even the holy hermit's solitary prospect of paradisical bliss, is but the glitter of a northern sun rising over a frozen region!! Compared with the many pleasures, the nameless raptures, we owe to the lovely QUEENS OF THE HEARTS OF MEN!!!

to Miss Helen Craik, 9 August 1790

Woman is the blood-royal of life; let there be slight degrees of precedency among them, but let them all be sacred.

to Miss Deborah Duff Davies, 6 April 1793

The mob of fashionable Female Youth, what are they? ... They prattle, laugh, sing, dance, finger a lesson, or perhaps turn over the pages of a fashionable Novel; but are their minds stored with any information worthy of the noble powers of reason and judgement; or do their hearts glow with sentiment, ardent, generous, and humane?

to Miss Jean McMurdo, July 1793

Writing

I am sick of writing where my bosom is not strongly interested.

to Mrs Dunlop, 12 February 1788

I have not a doubt but that the knack, the aptitude to learn the Muse's trade, is a gift bestowed by Him 'who forms the secret bias of the soul' [Aikenside *Pleasures of Imagination*, slightly misquoted]: but I as firmly believe that <u>excellence</u> in the profession is the fruit of industry, labour, attention, and pains – at least I am resolved to try my doctrine by the test of experience.

to Dr John Moore, 4 January 1789

I have no great faith in the boastful pretensions to intuitive propriety and unlaboured elegance. The rough material of Fine Writing is certainly the gift of Genius; but I as firmly believe that the workmanship is the united efforts of Pains, Attention and repeated Trial!

to Henry Erskine, 22 January 1789

Not that I am in haste for the Press ... I am aware that though I were to give to the world Performances superior to my former works, if they were productions of the same kind, the comparative reception they would meet with would mortify me. For this reason, I wish still to secure my old friend, Novelty, on my side, by the <u>kind</u> of my performances.

to Lady Elizabeth Cunningham, 23 December 1789

Coda: Lord Byron on Burns

What an antithetical mind! – tenderness, roughness –
delicacy, coarseness – sentiment, sensuality – soaring
and grovelling, dirt and deity – all mixed up in that one
compound of inspired clay!

    Journal, 13 December 1813

Glossary

aboon, aboun: above
ae: one
a-gley: awry
aiblins: perhaps
aince: once
air: early
airn: iron
auld: old
ava: at all
awa: away

barm: yeast
baudrons: cat
baukie-bird: bat
bawbee: halfpenny
bawsn't: brindled, having a white
    stripe down the face

beld: bald
belyve: quickly, at once
beuk: book
bicker'd: rushed, scurried
bield: protection, shelter
billy,-ies: fellow, lad
birkie: lively, spry fellow
blaudin: beating
bowsing: drinking heavily
brae: hill
brankie: finely dressed
brash: a sudden illness
braw: fine, splendid
brent: smooth, unwrinkled
brig: bridge
browster: brewer
brunstane: brimstone
bure the gree: came off best

ca': call
callan: stripling, lad
canny,-ie: shrewd, frugal
canty,-ie: lively, cheerful
carmagole: rascal
chap: knock
chaumer: chamber
chiel,-d: lad, young fellow

claes: clothes
clarty: dirty
clash: chatter, gossip
claut: grip
clink: jingle
Clootie: the Devil
clouts: clothes
cogg,-ie: wooden vessel for
    drinking
collieshangie: dispute, uproar
coof: fool, lout
cootie: tub
corbie: raven
countra: country
crancreuch: hoar frost
crap: top, head
creel: wicker basket
crooded: coo-ed
crously: merrily
cushat: wood-pigeon
cutty-sark: short shirt, chemise

dang: knocked
daur: dare
deil-haet: devil a bit
ding: knock
dinna: do not
doited: muddled, crazed
douce: sedate, sober
dought: was able, had the
    courage to do something
doup-skelper: lecher
downa: cannot
doylt: dazed, muddled
druke: soak, drench
drumlie: cloudy, gloomy
duddies: clothes
dyke: wall

een: eyes
eldritch: uncanny, unearthly

fae: foe
fash: bother, trouble
fause: false
faute,-or: fault, defaulter
feck: value; majority
fell: cruel, harsh
fier,-e: hearty, comrade

Glossary

fock: folk
fud: backside
fyle: defile, foul

gae,-d: go, went
gang: go
gangrel: vagrant, tramp
gar: make, cause
gash: shrewd, witty
gate: road, way
gaud: iron bar
gaunted: gaped, gasped
gawsie: ample, jovial-looking
gie,-d: give, gave
gilpey: young girl
gleg: quick, lively, smart
gloaming: twilight, dusk
gowd: gold
gowdspink: goldfinch
grain'd: groaned
grap'd: groped
gree: social degree, supremacy
greet: weep, cry
gulravage: romp, uproar

hae: have
haet: hot
hag(g): scar in moors made by
    water or peat cutting
hairst: harvest
half-lin: half-grown farmer's boy
halesome: wholesome
haly: holy
hansel: New-Year, Good-Luck
    gift
hap: cover, shield
hash: hack, waste
het: hot, excited
hinnie: sweetheart, darling
hizzie: wench
hurdies: buttocks, backside

ilk: each, every
ingle-neuk: chimney-corner

jad: wench, hussy
jaup: splash
jo: sweetheart
jouk: dodge

keekit: peeped
ken,-t: know, knew
kennin: little, trifle
kittle: tickle, excite
kintra: country
kirk: church
knappin-hammer: hammer for
    breaking stones

lade: load
lallans: Lowland Scots
lang-kent: familiar
lave: rest, remainder
laverock: lark
lawin: tavern-bill, reckoning
lear: learning, lore
leeze: delight by
lent: given, granted
libbet: castrated
licht: light
linkan: tripping, skipping
linn: waterfall
lint-white: white as flax
loe: love
loon: fellow
loove: love
lowe: flame
lug: ear, draw out
luggie: wooden dish with handles
lyart: grizzled

mair: more
maukins: hare
mauna: must not
mirk: darkness
mony: many
mottie: dusty
muir: moor

nappy: ale
naur: near
nit: nut

o'er: over
o'ergang: overcome
onie: any
orra: odd, extra
owre: over, too

paidle: paddle, wade

191

Glossary

pairt(r)ick: partridge
parritch: porridge
penny-wheep: small beer
pin: skewer
plack: small coin, copper
pleugh: plough
poortith: poverty
pou: pull
prent: print
puir: poor

quine: young girl

rade: rode
rape: rope
raploch: coarse, homely
rattan: rat
raxan,-in: stretching
reck the rede: take heed of advice
rickle: pile, stack of sheaves
rig: ridge
rin: run
row,-e: roll, wrap
rowth: abundance
rung: cudgel
rupit: husky, hoarse

sae: so
sair: sad, serve, treat
saugged: earthed up
saut: salt
scaith: hurt, damage
scow'r: roister, run
shaw: small wood
sheugh: ditch
sic: such
skaith: hurt
skelp: slap, strike
skelvy: ledged
sklent: slanted, squint
skouth: scope, liberty
skyte: a sudden blow
smoored: smothered
snaw-broo: slush
sonsie: buxom, comely
soup: sup
sowter: shoe-maker, cobbler
speel: climb
splore: frolic, uproar

sprechl'd: clambered
stang: stake
stark: strong, hardy
staw: over-feed, stuff
stock: plant, stem
stowe: cram, stuff
sturt: fret, trouble
styme, (see a): see at all
sugh: rushing sound of wind
swat: sweated
syne: since

tack: leasehold
tae: too
tak tent: take heed
tapsalteerie: topsy-turvy
tassie: goblet
thack: thatching
thole: endure, suffer
thowe: thaw
thraw: turn, twist
thrissle: thistle
tine,-t: lose, lost
tippeny: cheap ale
tirl'd: rattled (at the door)

unco: odd, strange
usquebae: whisky

vend: sell, utter

wad: would
wark: work
wauken,-in: awake
waur: worse
weel: well
whatna (on, by): what
whid: move noiselessly
whunstane: whinrock
wight: creature, strong, coarse
willie-waught: good big drink
winna: will not
wit: know
wrack: torment, punishment

yett: gate
yill: ale
yird: earth
yiska: hiccup